MILWAUKEE & MORE

A Guide To All The Things You Want To Do For Ages 1-99

By
Pamela Nonken, Nancy Luck & Barbara Smilow

Northword
P.O. Box 5634
Madison, Wisconsin 53705

Copyright © 1985 by Pamela Nonken, Nancy Luck & Barbara Smilow

All rights reserved. No part of this book may be reproduced in any form or by any means without the written consent of the publisher.

Library of Congress Cataloging in Publication Data
Luck, Nancy, 1944-
   Milwaukee & more.

   Includes index.
   1. Milwaukee (Wis.)—Description—Guide-books.
2. Milwaukee Region (Wis.)—Description and travel—
3. Wisconsin—Description and travel—1981- —
Guide-books. I. Nonken, Pamela, 1943-   . II. Smilow,
Barbara, 1938-   . III. Title. IV. Title:
Milwaukee & more.
F589.M63L83   1985   917.75'950443   85-7316
ISBN 0-942802-09-8 (pbk.)

Cover photo copyright © 1985 by Scott Witte.

Edited by Sue Whitcomb McCoy.

Designed and typeset by Jane Rundell Typography.

Cover design by Gryphon Studio.

Printed in the United States of America by George Banta Company, Inc.

"A Walk in the City" walking tours, maps, and illustrations reproduced courtesy of the Library Council of Metropolitan Milwaukee.

Bicycle tour maps and "Parks at a Glance" chart reproduced courtesy of the Milwaukee County Department of Parks, Recreation and Culture.

First printing 1985.

Contents

1. **Old Milwaukee** 1
   - Museums 2
   - Architectural Delights and Historical Sights 14
   - Religious Sites 21
2. **Tour the Town** 24
   - Commercial Tours 25
   - Driving and Walking Tours 27
   - A Walk in the City 29
   - Behind the Scenes 54
3. **Back to Nature** 62
4. **The Sporting Life** 71
   - Spectator Sports 72
   - Participation Sports 75
5. **Entertainment** 87
   - Ethnic Festivals 89
   - Music 96
   - Theater 100
   - The Rest 104
   - Tried It All? 109
6. **Eclectic Shopping** 111
   - Great Groceries 112
   - Bargains 116
   - Browsing 118
7. **Family Dining** 123
8. **Escape from Milwaukee** 130
9. **Index** 145

Preface

As creative and inquisitive mothers, we were continually exchanging ideas for touring, playing, and exploring in Milwaukee. From these informal exchanges, this book developed. A conventional tourist guide just wouldn't do. The nuance of Milwaukee is subtle and delightful. It is our intention to share what we found with you.

We welcome your suggestions, compliments, and criticisms. Send them to: Northword, P.O. Box 5634, Madison, Wisconsin 53705.

We greatly appreciate all the people who provided us with the information needed to compile *Milwaukee & More*. Our job was made easier and more enjoyable by their willingness to answer our numerous questions.

We especially thank the following people and organizations for their encouragement, suggestions, and materials: Robert J. Mikula, Milwaukee County Department of Parks, Recreation and Culture; William R. Drew, Greg Coenen, and Martha Brown, City of Milwaukee/Department of City Development; Archie A. Sarazin and Mary O'Hara Stacy, Performing Arts Center; Holiday Folk Fair; International Institute of Milwaukee County; and Janis Trilby and Carol Engel, Library Council of Metropolitan Milwaukee.

We thank all of our children — Aviva, Tamara, Talia, Arik, Aaron Jacob, Melissa, Marilyn, David, Lisa, and Marc — for whom this book was necessary. We are grateful for their enthusiasm and understanding. Special thanks go to Marilyn for her hours of typing, to Marc for his computer expertise, and to Melissa for her merciless proofreading.

We also thank our husbands — Harold, Gary and Michael — whose patience and understanding made this book possible.

Pamela Nonken, Nancy Luck & Barbara Smilow
Milwaukee, Wisconsin
January 1985

Before You Go

Plan ahead. It's the best way to ensure the success of your next outing, whether you go around the corner or across town. Our idea-packed book will help you enjoy Milwaukee to its fullest. It doesn't matter if you're a local or a globe-trotter, this guidebook makes touring easy. We've included hundreds of suggestions, possibilities, and insider tips that will appeal to both adults and kids. Hours, fees, and locations are listed, but are subject to change. Phone ahead to check before you go.

▶ The area code for Milwaukee and surrounding counties is 414. If no area code is listed, the code is 414.

Emergency Telephone Numbers

Ambulance, City of Milwaukee (Rescue Squad)	347-2323
Ambulance, your area	
Coast Guard (Marine and Air Emergency)	291-3165
If no answer, call	1-800-321-4400
Fire Department, City of Milwaukee	347-2323
Fire Department, your area	
Poison Center	931-4114
Police, City of Milwaukee	765-2323
Police, your area	

General Information

Newspapers and Magazine Calendars of Events

Community Newspapers (weekly)	764-0606
The Milwaukee Journal "Accent" Section (Thursday, Friday, and Sunday)	224-2000
Milwaukee Sentinel "Let's Go" section (Friday)	224-2000
Shinners Publications (weekly)	786-0600
Milwaukee Magazine (monthly)	273-1101

Recorded Messages and Important Numbers

Box Offices (see Chapter 5)	
Dial-A-Poem	372-7636
Funline of Events	799-1177
MECCA (Milwaukee Exposition and Convention Center and Arena)	271-2750
Milwaukee County	
Department of Parks, Recreation and Culture	278-4345
Extension Service	257-5300
Extension Service (horticulture and home economics)	257-5358
Parks Sports Office	645-8228
Sheriff (how to get from here to there)	278-4700
Transit System	344-6711

The Milwaukee Journal Public Service Desk
(information, pamphlets, books, etc.) 244-2120
The Milwaukee Journal/Sentinel Promotion Department 224-2427
Shoots 'n' Roots 224-4866
Time 844-1414
Tourism
    Department of City Development 223-5790
    Milwaukee Convention and Visitors Bureau 273-7222
    Wisconsin Division of Tourism 1-800-372-2737
Weather
    Recorded Message 936-1212
    National Weather Service 744-8000
    Wisconsin State Highway Patrol 785-4700
Wisconsin Outdoors Information (skiing, fishing, etc.) 799-1300

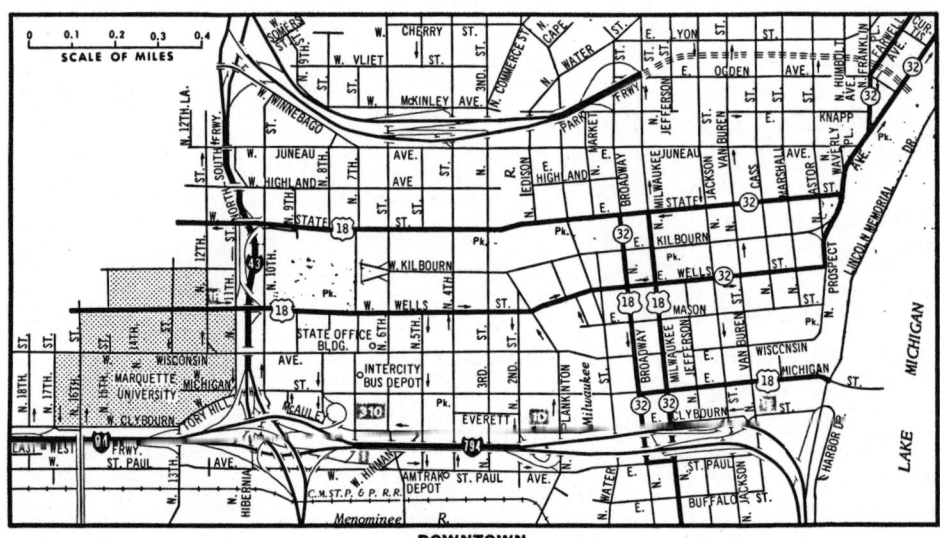

DOWNTOWN
MILWAUKEE

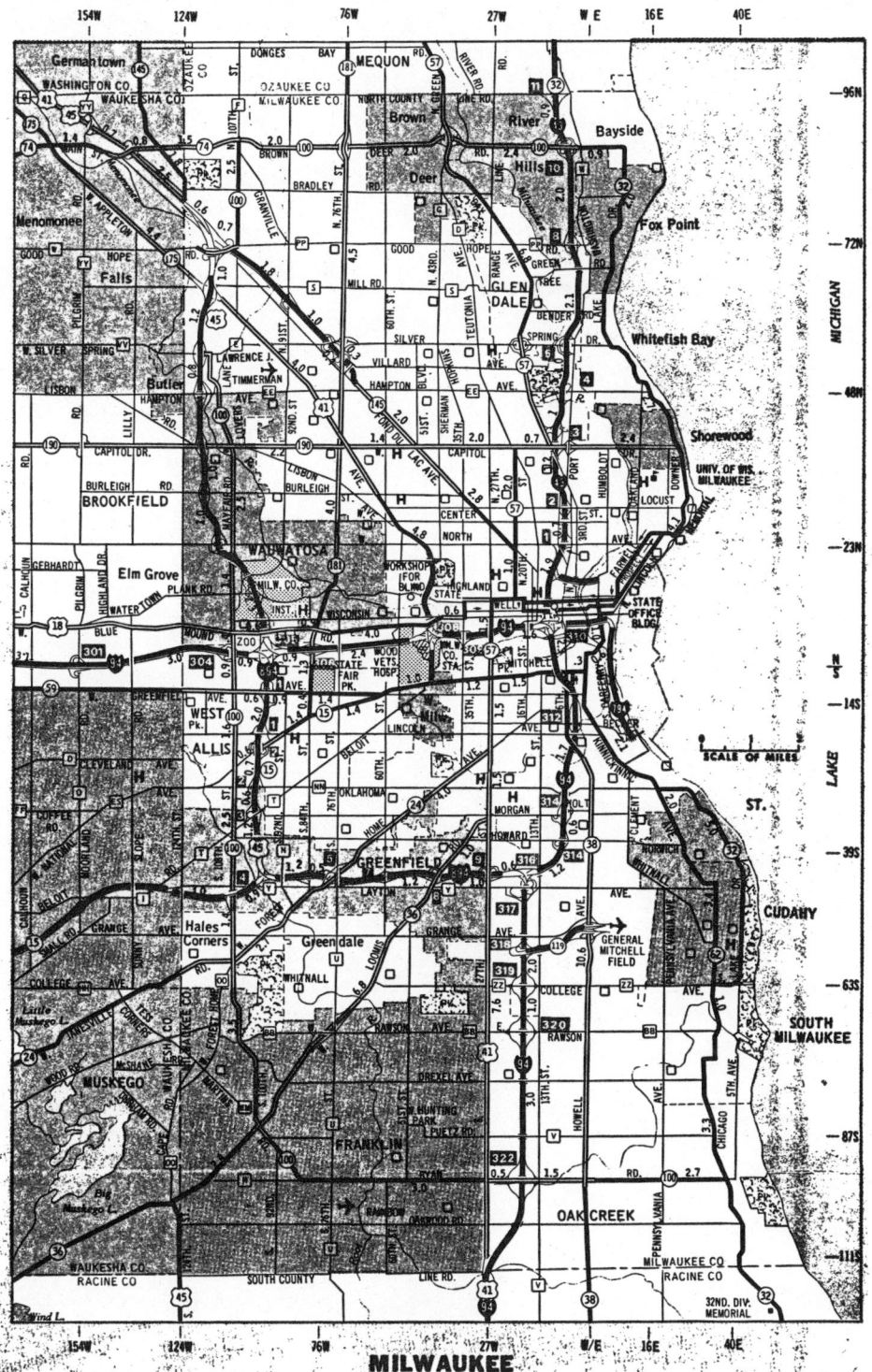

1
Old Milwaukee

Museums

Don't Overlook the Small Museums

These treasures are scattered all over our city and the surrounding territory, and are well worth the time it takes to find them. The dedicated curators and volunteers are your neighbors and friends, fellow Milwaukeeans who are anxious to preserve and share local history. They can tell some fascinating tales. You'll rarely hear a canned speech.

Art Museum—Milwaukee

750 North Lincoln Memorial Drive (271-9508).
On the Lakefront, Downtown.

- Open Tuesday, Wednesday, Friday, Saturday 10am-5pm; Thursday noon-9pm; Sunday 1-6pm; closed Monday.
- Admission, fee; children under 12, free; Milwaukee County residents with identification, free on Wednesday and Saturday 10 am-noon.
- Public tours are held most Sundays January-April with the admission price included in the cost of the tour. Group tours must be scheduled two weeks in advance.
- Parking lot south of the building, fee.
- Food service available at "The Buffet on the Lake" or snack bar in the south entrance stairwell; picnicking on the grounds by/in the sculpture. Also, see "Jazzy Lunches" in Chapter 5.
- Fine gift shop featuring works by Wisconsin artists.
- Handicapped accessibility and parking at east entrance only; tours for the hearing impaired may be arranged by calling in advance.

Designed by Eero Saarinen (1957), this contemporary museum takes advantage of its magnificent site on the Lakefront. The museum has a diverse collection that includes traditional and contemporary paintings, sculpture, and furniture. The Haitian collection is one of the largest in the world; enjoy the vivid colors and rhythm of composition.

Stop at the "Art Machine" at the entrance to the main gallery; our kids spent hours creating colorful designs and patterns. The "Janitor" (1973, Duane Hanson) is so realistic it's easy to walk past him and not realize he is an exhibit. Don't miss the "Magic Theatre." We were entranced with the thousands of sparkling lights and the eerie illusion of outer space.

Inquire about classes for children and adults. The members' newsletter and calendar provides information about film series, concerts, and lectures.

Here are some of our favorite events sponsored by the Art Museum.

▶ **Lakefront Festival of the Arts**
Lakefront, Art Museum grounds.
This large juried art show is held in mid-June. Paintings, crafts, demonstrations, food, and entertainment enhance an early summer weekend. Browse and buy. Admission, fee.

► **Bradley Sculpture Garden Tour**
2141 West Brown Deer Road (352-9156).

Picture Mrs. Harry Lynde Bradley sitting on her patio, directing the placement of these immense pieces of sculpture. She would have them moved and tilted and tipped this way and that until finally the exact positioning was pleasing to her. Now, you can view her contemporary sculptures in this exquisite setting of rolling terrain and groves of trees. You can even commune with the life-sized purple-spotted cows gathered around the pond if you like. The sculpture garden is rarely open to the public, so this once-a-year August afternoon is an experience that isn't duplicated anywhere else in the country. What we like best about the garden is the amount of space given each sculpture. Bring a picnic supper or purchase gourmet goodies there. Contact the Art Museum for the date and cost. Proceeds benefit the Art Acquisition Fund.

► **Film Series**
There are a number of series throughout the year, including Reel Art, Film (visual and performing arts) and the latest series for children. All are scheduled on weekends (see Chapter 5).

Bodamer Log Cabin Museum

South 56th Street and West Layton Avenue, Greenfield (543-3324).
- Open May-October Sunday 2-4:30 pm.
- Admission, free.
- Parking nearby.

This log cabin (1833) was actually hidden away under layers of lathe, plaster and clapboard siding. Over the years, it had acquired an additional 1½ stories, with added rooms and porches, until the original structure was unrecognizable. In 1966, the Greenfield Historical Society began restoration work on the structure. The original logs were found to be as sound as when they were first put in place. Today, the reconstructed cabin stands on a lovely new site and is furnished as it was in pioneer days. Imagine using some of those old kitchen utensils! The Greenfield Historical Society is also restoring a Cream City brick cottage on this site. Watch for the Heritage Days Celebration held in mid-September; it's a great time to visit.

Brooks Stevens Automotive Museum

10325 North Port Washington Road, Mequon (241-4185).
I-43 to Port Washington Road exit; north one mile.

- Open daily 10am-5pm; call for holiday hours.
- Admission, fee; discount for groups of 10 or more.
- Guided tours may be arranged (241-3800).
- Parking lot.
- Picnic tables are on the grounds; there are restaurants nearby.

This informal museum attempts to open seven days a week. If you find the doors closed, look for the guide, who will be happy to show you around. There's a lot to see: everything from a 1904 Cadillac to a late-model Excalibur. You'll see Al Jolson's 1927 Mercedes-Benz, King Farouk's 1949 Rolls Royce, and Harry Truman's Lincoln limousine. Watch for the annual MG-sponsored sportscar show after Labor Day. No special facilities but staff glad to aid handicapped.

Cedar Lake Campus "House of Friendship"

Highway Z, 2 miles south of Highway 33, in the town of West Bend (414/276-4370).

- Open Sunday 2-6pm.
- Admission, free.

Rooms from an antique farmhouse have been recreated here. Farm implements, clothing and period furnishings date from the 1800s. In the summer, the old-time schoolhouse is open for classes. On permanent display is a hospital room which features vintage medical equipment.

Charles Allis Art Museum

1801 North Prospect Avenue (278-8295).
Entrance at 1630 East Royall Place.

- Open Wednesday-Sunday 1-5pm, Wednesday evening 7-9pm; closed Monday, Tuesday, and holidays.
- Admission, free.
- Call in advance for tours.
- Parking on the street.
- Wheelchair access may be arranged.

This house is a real jewel! Charles Allis, one of Milwaukee's early tycoons, built this Tudor home in 1909-1910 to house his treasures, with the intent of leaving the house and his collections to the residents of Milwaukee. The house was designed by architect Alexander Eschweiler and is furnished much as it was during the years Allis and his wife lived here. Look up as you enter to see the three-tiered stained glass window by Louis Comfort Tiffany which echoes the hues of the marblework nearby. The art collection throughout the house includes French and American landscape paintings from the 19th century, fine antique furniture, jade, cloisonne, and small bronzes. The world-famous Chinese porcelains date from 300 B.C. to the 18th century. Look for the teapot without a top (it's in the bottom!). Local collections are exhibited monthly. (Special events feature Wisconsin artists.) There is a juried Wisconsin Handweaver's show in November, and in December, each room is decorated for Christmas. Watch the newspapers for special events and concerts during the year.

The facilities offer a lovely setting for private functions. Call for rental information.

Colnik Museum

531 North Eighth Street (272-0381).

- Open by appointment only.
- Admission, donation.
- Group tours for 18-20 people; tea and cake served.

Cyril Colnik was Milwaukee's premier ironworks craftsman. Why not visit his home/studio? Gretchen Colnik, his daughter, will be your personal guide and show you the collection that has been donated to the City of Milwaukee.

Dousman-Dunkel-Behling House (project in progress)

1135 North Pilgrim Road, Elm Grove.

Imagine a stagecoach traveling along a plank road, pulling up to the front of an inn and unloading the luggage from its topside onto the second-story porch of the inn. This was a familiar scene in 1843 when the Dousman house stood at the corner of Bluemound and Pilgrim roads, halfway between Milwaukee and Waukesha along the Watertown Plank Road. The Elmbrook Historical Society has undertaken the restoration of this lovely home to its 1860 appearance. The hardware, woodwork and banisters are all original; only the kitchen has been remodeled. There's a "Ladies' Room" (where the women passengers waited while the men refreshed themselves in the "Bar Room"), as well as "Wayfarers' Rooms" and the "Family Rooms." The woodwork and furniture in the house were handcrafted by itinerant cabinetmakers who passed through Wisconsin.

Germantown Historical Museum

Highway 145 and Holy Hill and Maple roads; in the Christ Church, one mile east of Highway 41 on Holy Hill Road.

- Open during the summer Sundays 1-4pm.

This 122-year-old church is listed on the National Register of Historic Places. Local history is lovingly preserved in this small museum. Included in its collection are more than 400 photos of early area residents. The microfilm records are a find for local genealogists: There are some 5,000 indexed surnames.

A good time to visit is mid-October when antique engines and other machinery are on display in the front yard during the Fall Festival.

Greene Memorial Museum

3367 North Downer Avenue (963-4794, 963-4561).
On the campus of the University of Wisconsin-Milwaukee.

- Open Monday and Wednesday 9am-noon and by special appointment; closed during Christmas break.
- Admission, free.
- Group tours are especially well-suited for children.
- Park where you can and read the signs carefully for the time limits; good access by public transportation.

The rocks from right under us are here at this geological museum. The agates and Devonian fossils were all found in the Milwaukee area. Children can enjoy hands-on experience here. There are samples of rocks, minerals and fossils for them to pick up and touch, and there's also a six-inch Tyrannosaurus Rex tooth. The model of a giant winged reptile suspended from the ceiling is a point of interest too. Requests for special presentations are encouraged by the accommodating staff.

Also see "University of Wisconsin-Milwaukee" in Chapter 5.

Haggerty Museum of Art

Twelfth Street at Wisconsin Avenue (224-7290).
On the mall between Wisconsin Avenue and Clybourn Street; three buildings south of Wisconsin Avenue.

- Open Monday-Friday 10am-4:30pm, Saturday noon-4:30pm, Sunday noon-5pm; closed December 24-25 and January 1-2.
- Admission, free.
- Public parking.
- Handicapped accessibility.

The vertical thrust and angular planes of this expansive structure were created to house the art collection of Marquette University. There is a broad scope to this collection which represents nearly 100 years of art donations. The works of art have been installed with a concern for their impact, resulting in an exciting relationship of one work to another. The cornerstone of this collection is the Bible series of 105 hand-colored etchings by Marc Chagall donated by Patrick and Beatrice Haggerty.

Heg Museum

6300 Heg Park Road, Wind Lake (414/895-2700).
Highway 36 south of Milwaukee, through Wind Lake.

- Open Saturday and Sunday 1-5pm Memorial Day through September.
- Admission, free.

The museum is in a two-room log cabin built in 1837. The cabin was moved to its present location in the 1920s and has been furnished in pioneer decor. The museum is a memorial to Colonel Hans Heg and the regiment of Norwegians he recruited to fight in the Civil War, and features Norwegian and Civil War artifacts.

Heritage Museum-Boy Scout Council Office

3716 West Wisconsin Avenue (344-6830).

- By appointment only.
- Admission, fee.
- Arrange tours 1 week in advance.

Since 1910 when Boy Scouting began, this museum has been collecting Scout memorabilia. You'll find uniforms, photos and rare books.

Historical Center—Milwaukee County

910 North Third Street (273-8288).

- Open Monday 9:30am-5pm, Saturday 10am-5pm, Sunday 11am-5pm; closed major holidays.
- Admission, free.
- Guided tours for groups; call 2 weeks in advance to make an appointment. Group tour admission, fee.
- Park on the street or in one of the commercial lots in the area.
- Handicapped accessibility on the first floor only.

As you go west across the Kilbourn Avenue Bridge, you'll have an unobstructed view of this graceful historic building. Housed in a landmark bank (1913), this Milwaukee County museum features horse-drawn and early fire-fighting equipment. Children will enjoy the old-fashioned drugstore. Among other exhibits is a "Blacks in Milwaukee" display. In September, the museum presents a costumed reenactment of the Revolutionary War in Pere Marquette Park.

▶ Special feature: Genealogical Research Library. Open Monday-Friday 9:30am-noon and 1-4:30pm.

Jeremiah Curtin House (project in progress)

8600 West Grange Avenue (273-8288).
In the village of Greendale.

Jeremiah Curtin's family lived in two log cabins before building this traditional Irish cottage and springhouse in 1846. The limestone home will soon be opened to the public by the Milwaukee County Historical Society.

Kalvelage Schloss

2432 West Kilbourn Avenue (425-3510).
Exit I-94 at 26th Street to Kilbourn Avenue; travel 2 blocks east.

- Open by appointment only.
- Admission, fee; children under 6, free.
- Group tours by appointment.
- Parking on the street.

The on-going restoration of this home is the result of loving efforts by its current owner. (At this time, only the first floor is open to the public.) Ornate paneling by the Matthews Brothers and wrought-iron balconies and railings by Cyril Colnik reflect fine Milwaukee craftsmanship. Joseph Kalvelage commissioned Otto Strack, the architect of the Pabst Theatre, to design this German Baroque, French Renaissance home (1898). It has been used intermittently as a hospital and a rooming house, yet has remained structurally unchanged. The collection of the Milwaukee Musical Arts Center is here and includes the pipe organ from the Milwaukee Auditorium, music boxes, pianos and organs from 1835-1935. Ask for a demonstration of the novelty mechanical musical instruments.

Kilbourntown House

On Estabrook Parkway, just north of Capitol Drive; in Estabrook Park.

- Open during the summer Tuesday, Thursday, Saturday 10am-5pm, Sunday 1pm-5pm; closes for the season on Labor Day.
- Admission, free.

This temple-type Greek Revival house, built by carpenter Benjamin Church (1844), was moved to its present site from Kilbourntown, one of Milwaukee's original settlements. The furnishings reflect the decor of its time. The Doric columns and exterior walls of hand-hewn beams and Cream City brick lend a feeling of strength to the structure. During restoration, three fireplaces were uncovered, in the kitchen, dining room, and parlor.

    Watch the newspapers for announcements about the special happenings; our families love the ice-cream socials, held the last Sunday in June, 2-4 pm.

Lowell Damon House

2107 North Wauwatosa Avenue, Wauwatosa 53213 (273-8288).
(76th Street and Wauwatosa Avenue are the same in Wauwatosa.)

- Open Wednesday 3pm-5pm, Sunday 1pm-5pm.
- Admission, free.
- Group tours are available for school age and older, maximum group size 40 people; call or write in advance.

The Lowell Damon House, built in the 1840s, is a lovely example of New England architecture. Most of the furniture was donated by Wauwatosa residents and dates from 1700 to 1900. Particularly charming is the children's room. On a nice day, you are welcome to picnic in the garden.

Milwaukee County Public Museum

800 West Wells Street (278-2700).

- Open daily 9am-5pm; closed Thanksgiving and Christmas.
- Admission, fee; Milwaukee County residents with identification, free on Saturday and Sunday 9am-10:30am; handicapped and children under 3, free.
- Call in advance for information about group tours.
- There are commercial lots in the area; the entrance to the municipal lot is on Seventh Street.
- Cafeteria in the lower level.
- Gift shop. (It's worth a good browse; save some time for it.)
- Strollers and wheelchairs are available at the security desk; handicapped accessibility.

You'll feel as though you're part of the exhibits as you stroll through the Streets of Old Milwaukee. You can examine the exacting details of the houses in the European Village and explore your ethnic roots. Children delight in the realistic portrayal of animals displayed in their natural habitats. (See Tyrannosaurus Rex munching on Triceratops Stegosaurus.) Neophyte naturalists won't want to miss the poisonous mushroom identification exhibit. You can bring the kids back once a month to swap and barter old treasures for new at the Trading Post.

Are you free this summer? Here's a special dinosaur opportunity: Ask about the summer "Dig a Dinosaur Expedition" in Jensen, Utah. Call the curator of paleontology for the details (278-2740).

Also see "Kite Flying" in Chapter 4 and "Films" in Chapter 5.

Muskego Town Hall Museum

S 8200 Racine Avenue, Muskego.

- Open the third Sunday of each month 1pm-4:30pm.
- Admission, fee.

The exhibits here recall Muskego farm life at the turn of the century. The farmhouse is the original structure built in 1880. A collection of old hand tools and machinery is featured in the museum.

Oak Creek Historical Society Museum

15th Street and Forest Hill Avenue, Oak Creek.
* Open during the summer Sunday 2pm-4pm.
* Admission, free.

This small museum preserves local heritage.

Old Falls Village Museum

County Line and Pilgrim roads, Menomonee Falls (251-5177).
* Open during the summer May 1 through September, Sunday 1pm-4pm.
* Admission, fee; children under 6, free.
* Special tours may be arranged year-round by appointment.

Get a sense of a town's beginnings. Tour the restored log cabin (1856), the first schoolhouse in Menomonee Falls (1851), a railroad depot (1890) and a carriage house with old fire trucks and sleighs. The National Register of Historic Places has listed the Miller-Davidson limestone house and barn (1858). Annual events include an ice-cream social the third Sunday in July and a Christmas tea the first Sunday in December.

Old World Wisconsin

See "Eagle" in Chapter 6.

Pabst Mansion

2000 West Wisconsin Avenue (931-0808).
* Open Monday-Saturday 10am-4pm, last tour at 3:15pm; Sunday noon-3:30pm, last tour at 2:30pm; closed weekdays January and February except for group tours; closed major holidays.
* Admission, fee; children under 6, free.
* Call in advance for group tours and special rates.
* Limited parking behind the building.

If you've ever wondered how the wealthy lived in the early days of Milwaukee, the Pabst Mansion presents a story of opulence and splendor. Frederick Pabst came to America at the age of 12 and began his maritime career as a cabin boy on a Great Lakes steamer. At the age of 26, he married Maria Best and eventually became president of his father-in-law's brewery. The mansion was built in 1893 at a cost of over $255,000, at a time when carpenters earned 35¢ per hour. This 37-room home, with its 12 baths and 14 fireplaces, features sumptuously carved woodwork by the Matthews Brothers and priceless ornamental ironwork by Cyril Colnik, as well as carved panels imported from a seventeenth-century Bavarian castle. The docents are special; they really make the tour interesting. The Sugar Plum Days during the first three weekends in December draw the largest crowds of the year; call for details. You can also inquire about renting the mansion for your next social affair!

Pioneer Village of Ozaukee County

Highway I west of Fredonia (414/692-9910).
North edge of Hawthorne Hills County Park.

- Open first Sunday in June until second Sunday in October, Wednesday and Sunday noon-5pm.
- Admission, fee; children under 6, free.
- Group tours (414/242-0587).
- Ample parking.
- Lunches available in the Hawthorne Hills Clubhouse south of the village; picnicking in the park east of the village along the Milwaukee River; no food allowed in the village.

Once again we can credit residents for preserving their local history. In 1961 the Ozaukee County Historical Society determined to save the Michael Ahner house (1850), which was about to be torn down. As it turned out, that was just the beginning, and now an entire village has been restored. Thirteen buildings have been furnished as they were between 1840 and 1860. The Trading Post, Carpenter Shop, and Blacksmith Shop are full of original tools-of-the-trade. Even the flowers and trees have been carefully selected and planted for their historic authenticity. On Sundays the village has a lived-in look. "Pioneers" in period clothing demonstrate log-trimming, weaving, iron-working, and bread-making. Don't pass by the Daiger House without a look at the Country Store inside, where you can purchase wooden whistles, sunbonnets, and more.

Trimborn Farm Park (project in progress)

8801 West Grange Road (332-PARK).
Near Whitnall Park and the Root River Parkway.

The Park People have a pet project in progress. They are helping the Milwaukee County Department of Parks, Recreation, and Culture restore and develop this National Register historic property.

Trimborn Farm is believed to be the only limestone facility that remains relatively intact in this state. For more than 50 years during the mid-nineteenth century it played a key role in the development of Milwaukee County by providing lime for building construction. Later the farm was converted into a major dairying facility. The grounds have been cleaned up and the 75-foot center kiln restored. The Cream City brick farmhouse is being renovated.

Be the first person on your block to visit our county's first historic park when it opens. In the meantime, visit Trimborn Farm at the beginning of September for the Harvest of Arts and Crafts.

Villa Terrace

2220 North Terrace Avenue (271-3656).
North Avenue east; right on Terrace Avenue at the top of the bluff, above Lake Michigan.

- Open September-May Wednesday, Saturday, Sunday 1pm-5pm; June-August Wednesday-Sunday 1pm-5pm.
- Admission, free.
- Call in advance to arrange group tours; inquire about tours personalized for your group by the Art Museum docents. Group tour admission, free.
- Rent Villa Terrace for occasions; call for information.
- Handicapped accessibility on the first floor only.

It's somewhat incongruous to find this sunny Mediterranean courtyard and villa on the bluffs of Lake Michigan. All the more delightful! This Italian Renaissance home (1923) was constructed by L.R. Smith, son of industrialist A.O. Smith. It is now a museum for the decorative arts under the auspices of the Milwaukee Art Museum. Woodwork by the Matthews Brothers (in the library), and ironwork by Cyril Colnik, grace this home designed by David Adler. Children and adults will enjoy finding the door painted on the hallway wall in deference to the architect's love of symmetry. The Smith children collected stones of certain sizes and colors from the beach for the mosaic floor in the courtyard. Stand for a moment at the top of the bluff and imagine how many trips you could manage lugging a load of stones!

▶ Special feature: Watch the newspapers for special events held here during the year. We've attended plays, a needlework show, an antique doll exhibit, private parties, and concerts here. Each event was enhanced by its surroundings in this lovely home. It's a perfect place to imagine yourself an indulged connoisseur.

Waukesha County Historical Museum

101 West Main Street (414/548-7186).
At the corner of Main Street and East Avenue.

- Open Monday-Friday 9am-4:30pm, Sunday 1-5pm.
- Admission, free.
- Group tours for 10-50 people; call 2 weeks in advance.
- Parking available in the municipal lot behind the stores.
- Handicapped accessibility by prior arrangement.

Waukesha celebrated its Sesquicentennial in 1984. Some of the original settlers were farmers who came for the fertile land, some were soda-water bottlers who came for the clear water. Mineral springs attracted those in search of "health-restoring" mud baths. The museum is on the site of an old Indian mound and features a large collection of arrowheads and pioneer artifacts. There is a fine exhibit of antique dolls and miniature rooms. If your ancestors settled in Waukesha County, it's easy to trace your roots; the Genealogy Collection here is very complete with naturalization papers, school records, diaries, and county documents. The "hands on" Old Toys Exhibit is a hit with the kids.

West Allis Historical Society Museum
8405 West National Avenue, 53227 (541-6970).
- Open Sunday 2pm-4pm, Tuesday 7pm-9pm, and by appointment.
- Admission, free; donations welcomed.
- Parking lot is to the west of the building.
- Handicapped accessibility.

This Richardson Romanesque Cream City brick building (1887) has something of interest for every age group. Exhibits include equipment from an old-time dental clinic, a schoolroom, Indian history, and a doll collection. You can ring the antique school bell and wander through the labelled herb garden (recipes available). The headstones in the old cemetery on the museum grounds are a record of the waves of immigrants who came to West Allis.

▶ Special feature: A walking tour of West Allis is available with a guide; call for an appointment. If you prefer a self-guided tour, send a self-addressed stamped envelope and 25¢ with your written request.

Winton-Sprengel House
19765 West National Avenue (542-3643).
In New Berlin's Prospect Hill Park.
- Open by appointment only.
- Picnic tables on the grounds.

Postmaster Louis Winton and his wife, Mary, built this home in 1870. They settled in the area called Prospect Hill where residents were Yankees from New England and New York. In addition to the restored home, there is a carriage house with a large collection of vehicles and a recreated country store.

Architectural Delights and Historical Sights

Cedar Creek Settlement

N70 W6340 Bridge Road, Cedarburg (377-8020).
I-43 to Cedarburg exit (County C); right on Washington Avenue to Bridge Road. Approximately 15 miles north of Milwaukee.

- Open Monday-Saturday 10am-5pm; Sunday noon-5pm.
- Call in advance for tour information.
- Parking on the streets nearby.
- There are several appealing eating establishments on the premises.
- Handicapped accessibility on the first floor only.

Cedar Creek Settlement features 20 charming specialty shops housed in a restored 1864 woolen mill. In some of the shops you'll find artists and craftspeople demonstrating their skills. As you go from shop to shop, you can touch the looms and shuttles standing in the hallways and try to figure out how they work. Call for information about the popular Stone Mill Winery tour (377-8020). There is plenty to do here for the better part of a day.

City Hall—Milwaukee

200 East Wells Street (278-2221).

- Open Monday-Friday 8am-4:45pm; closed Thanksgiving, Christmas, New Year's Day, Fourth of July.
- Admission, free.
- Guided tours by appointment only.
- Parking on the street; commercial lots available nearby.
- Handicapped accessibility to all floors.

This rejuvenated Flemish Renaissance-style landmark (1895) houses the Mayor's office. Let your eyes wander from the dramatic arches at street level to the focal point of this building, the bell tower. To see the attractively appointed Council Chambers, you'll have to take one of the guided tours. The City Clerk's office recommends this tour for high-schoolers and adults.

Di Suvero Sculpture

East Wisconsin Avenue at the Lakefront.

We won't attempt to describe it. You will love it or hate it, but you can't miss it!

First Wisconsin Center

777 East Wisconsin Avenue (765-4321).

- The observation deck on the 41st floor is open Monday-Friday 2pm-4pm; the Galleria and shops have varying hours.
- Admission, free.
- The entrance to the parking structure is on Michigan Avenue.
- In the Galleria, two restaurants and one fast-food service.
- Handicapped accessibility to the building, but not to the 41st floor.

The tallest building in Wisconsin provides a 360° panoramic view of Milwaukee. If you are at the Lakefront with a few minutes to spare, use them to see this new perspective of Milwaukee!

Forest Home Cemetery

2405 West Forest Home Avenue (645-2632).

- Open Monday-Friday 8am-4:30pm, Saturday 8:30am-noon. Stop at the office to pick up a map.
- Admission, free.

Gone are the days when heavy wagons filled with barrels of beer thundered along Milwaukee's cobblestone streets. Gone, too, are those barons whose beer made them and Milwaukee famous — Joseph Schlitz, Captain Frederick Pabst, Jacob Best and Valentine Blatz no longer sell their sudsy brews to company-owned corner bars. The final resting place for these giants in the brewing industry is Forest Home Cemetery, in a section designated Beer Corner. The Pabst memorial is marked by a short flight of steps; at the top sits a stone woman holding a funeral wreath. The Blatz mausoleum is a massive block building; the Schlitz memorial features an angel raising a hand skyward. These are impressive monuments — a measure of the wealth and influence that once was theirs.

The Grain Exchange

225 East Michigan Street (272-6230).

- Group tours for 40 or more people by appointment only; call 1-2 months in advance. Don't be discouraged if your group is small; it will be combined with another one.
- Admission, fee.
- Age 12 and older.
- Parking in commercial lots.

In the 1860s, Milwaukee was the country's largest exporter of wheat. That was the economic justification for building this extravagant and lavishly detailed grain exchange (1879). Banker Alexander Mitchell was the man of taste behind the project. The exterior styling is Second Empire-Italian Villa characterized by the mansard roof and clock tower. The real impact hits you when you enter the 10,000-square-foot grand trading room with its three-story "marble" columns, and decorative painted trim and ceiling panels which feature Wisconsin wild flowers. The mural, by Milwaukee artist John Conway, depicts three classical figures representing Trade, Industry, and Agriculture. (Notice the ticker-tape machine in their midst.) The models for the women in the mural were Milwaukee society ladies.

It's hard to picture this room with oats and wheat scattered on the floor, though it operated as a trading center for nearly 50 years. By 1935, the grain trade had diminished and the building was considered out-of-fashion. It was divided into office space and called the Mackie Building. Only through intensive restoration efforts, directed by Eleanor P. Ashley, has the grand trading room been returned to its original glory. The complexities of this restoration are the makings of a legend. The Tiffany stained glass, for example, turned up in a local pub and the murals were discovered beneath false ceilings.

The Grain Exchange is often rented for private affairs. If you receive an invitation to attend a function there, GO — it's spectacular!

Grand Avenue Mall

275 West Wisconsin Avenue (244-0384).

- Open Monday-Friday 10am-5pm, Saturday 10am-6pm, Sunday noon-5pm; closed Easter, Fourth of July, Thanksgiving, Christmas and New Year's Day.
- Parking structures are connected to the mall and are easily entered from Michigan and Plankinton Avenues; nominal fee.
- Varied food services available.
- Handicapped accessibility is at street level entrances and in the parking ramps at levels 1 and 5. Eleven elevators are located in the mall as well as in Boston Store and Gimbels.

We've never been there when it wasn't bustling. The people-watching is superb! This exciting retail center was designed by the Rouse Company and connects five historic buildings. The centerpiece is the restored Plankinton Arcade (1915-16) which combines the elegance of a by-gone era with the architectural styling of today. If you're hungry, there's a tempting variety of ethnic fast foods in the third floor Spiesegarten. There is also plenty of opportunity to nibble your way through the rest of the mall.

Northpoint Lighthouse

In Lake Park, on the bluff.

Look for the lighthouse near the bridge with the marvelous lions. The original Northpoint Lighthouse was built in 1837, but it's been replaced and moved around a bit. Once situated at the east end of Wisconsin Avenue, it was replaced in 1855 by a tower 100 feet east of the present location. (It had to be moved due to erosion of the bluff.) The navigational signal from the lighthouse is visible for 25 miles.

While you're in the area, you might wish to wander over to the bus "turn-around" near Locust Street and Lake Drive. There is an Indian Burial Mound nearby identified only by an inconspicuous marker on a rock.

Northpoint Watertower

North Avenue at the top of the bluff, above Lake Michigan.

This Victorian Gothic watertower (1873) is one of the few remaining structures of its type in the United States. Though it is no longer functioning, it is a sentimental landmark. The 175-foot limestone tower was once an integral part of the city's first water system. Some of Milwaukee's extravagant industrial barons once lived in this area. It's worth a stroll through the neighborhood to look at some of the elegant turn-of-the-century homes.

Old Smokey

South Bay and East Conway streets.

Can you picture 412 tons? Old Smokey was the last steam engine operated by The Milwaukee Road. It's a marvelous background for family photographs and a nostalgic sight for railroad buffs. This landmark is sitting on its site, waiting for you to visit.

Pabst Theatre

144 East Wells Street (Box Office 271-3773, Tours 271-4747).

- Guided tours are offered for 10 or more by appointment only; suitable for older children and adults.
- Admission, fee; student groups, free.
- Commercial parking lots in the area.
- Handicapped accessibility for the first floor only; headphones are available for the hearing impaired.

Don't wait for a performance: see the Pabst! This opulent Victorian Baroque landmark was built in 1895 by Captain Frederick Pabst, who spared no expense in elaborate ornamentation, stage facilities, audience accommodations or acoustics. He even included a basement tavern where men enjoyed a free sandwich and schooner of beer during the intermission (while the women waited in the lobby, of course). This recently restored theater offers an intimate setting for a variety of artistic performances throughout the year. A popular holiday attraction is the Milwaukee Repertory Theatre's production of Dickens' *A Christmas Carol.*

Pfister Hotel

424 East Wisconsin Avenue (273-8222).

If you find yourself on East Wisconsin Avenue for any reason, take a few minutes to stroll through the charming lobby of the Pfister Hotel (1890), with its gold-leaf ceilings, nineteenth-century art collection, and Victorian furnishings. Two bronze lions, donated by Timothy Anthony Chapman (of department-store fame), guard the stairway to the mezzanine.

The building of a fine hotel in Juneautown had been the dream of tanner Guido Pfister; his son, Charles, completed the project with the help of local businessmen. The Pfister is an example of what architectural historians call Richardson Romanesque — a kind of robust styling that became very popular in the 1880s and 1890s in Milwaukee. (Other fine examples are St. Paul's Episcopal Church and the Federal Building.)

Public Library System—Milwaukee

Central Library
814 West Wisconsin Avenue (278-3000).

- Open Monday-Thursday 8:30am-9pm, Friday-Saturday 8:30am-5:30pm; closed Sunday, Christmas, New Year's Day, Thanksgiving.
- Arrange group tours in advance.
- Commercial parking lots in the area.
- Book drop at drive-in window when library is closed.
- Handicapped accessibility.

The highlight of this classical building (1898) is the ornate marble rotunda. Pop into the lobby sometime, stand on the elaborate mosaic floor, and look up! Check out the used book sales; there are two each year. Call for dates and locations. Great buys, and the proceeds support the library system.

The Central Library offers the following special collections and services:

- Central Youth Library (278-3091). Open Monday-Thursday noon-8:30pm, Friday-Saturday 9am-5:30pm.
- Local History Room (278-3074) and Wisconsin Marine Historical Collection. Open Monday 12:30-9pm, Tuesday-Saturday 12:30-5:15pm.
- Regional Library for the Blind and Physically Handicapped. Open Monday-Friday 8:30am-5pm.
- Drive-in Service, 755 North Eighth Street (278-3000). Open Monday-Thursday 8:30am-6pm, Friday-Saturday 8:30am-5pm; closed Sunday.

Branch Libraries
The Public Library System includes the following branch libraries, all of which are open Monday-Thursday noon-8:30pm, Friday-Saturday 9am-5pm; closed Sunday.
- Atkinson, 1960 West Atkinson Avenue (278-3068).
- Capitol, 7413 West Capitol Drive (278-3006).
- Center Street, 2620 West Center Street (278-3090).
- East, 1910 East North Avenue (278-3058).
- Finney, 4243 West North Avenue (278-3066).
- Forest Home, 1432 West Forest Home Avenue (278-3083).
- Llewellyn, 907 East Russell Avenue (278-3019).
- Martin Luther King, 310 West Locust Street (278-3098).
- Mill Road, 6431 North 76th Street (278-3088).
- North Milwaukee, 3310 West Villard Avenue (278-3079).
- Oklahoma, 3501 West Oklahoma Avenue (278-3055). Also open Monday 9am-noon, Friday 5-8:30pm.
- Tippecanoe, 3912 South Howell Avenue (278-3085).

Science, Economics and Technology Center
814 West Wisconsin Avenue (765-9966).
In the Milwaukee Public Central Library.
- Open Tuesday-Saturday 9am-5pm, Sunday 1-5pm. On Sunday, use the Library entrance on Wisconsin Avenue.
- Admission, fee; group tours with reservations will receive a discount.
- The gift shop features goodies for science buffs.

The displays are designed to be touched, to educate and entertain at the same time. Magnets, motors, electricity and computers are just a few of the exhibits that dazzle and delight adults and children alike. Cavort in front of funhouse mirrors, whisper to each other across the room, manipulate your own shadow. Allow plenty of time; you'll find it hard to leave.

Tivoli Gardens (home of the Milwaukee Ballet Company)
504 West National Avenue (643-7677).
Located in the historic Walker's Point area.

- Tours are given Monday-Friday 9am-5pm; ages 12 and over; call ahead.
- Donations appreciated.
- Parking on the street.
- Handicapped accessibility on the first floor only.

Can you picture this structure as a fashionable beer garden? Tivoli Gardens (1901) was constructed as an open-air produce market and was later enclosed by the Schlitz Brewing Company. The original facade of this restored building is the entry to the Milwaukee Ballet Company. Call ahead and plan on touring during rehearsal times. You might even consider joining the United Performing Arts Fund (UPAF). Open House bus tour in January or February; for UPAF tour information call 273-7121.

The renovating of Tivoli Gardens by the Milwaukee Ballet Company was a bonus for the historic neighborhood of Walker's Point, where you'll also find unique little shops. We loved the Brasslight (719 South Fifth Street, 383-0675). If it seems closed, knock on the door; they love to show you around. Chip n' Pys' (815 South Fifth Street, 645-3435) is a chic cafe; it's easy to miss, so look for the place with a white piano in the window.

Ward Memorial Theatre/Liberace Playhouse (project in progress)
5000 West National Avenue (384-3848).
On the grounds of the Veterans Administration Medical Center.

Ward Memorial Theatre/Liberace Playhouse (1882) is the first stage in a restoration project undertaken by the Soldiers Home Foundation. Several of the 69 buildings on the grounds of the Veterans Administration Medical Center date from just after the Civil War. Corrine A. Perrine Harvey, widow of Governor Louis P. Harvey, visited President Abraham Lincoln three times in her efforts to establish a facility in Milwaukee for soldiers returning from the Civil War.

This Cream City brick building originally served as an amusement hall, chapel, restaurant, store and railway depot for returning soldiers. You can recognize it by its twin-gabled turrets, Tiffany stained-glass windows and spacious verandas. The playhouse reflects authentic American craftsmanship with hand-hewn beams, handcut square nails and rich oak woodwork.

Liberace grew up across the street from the Soldiers Home grounds and performed in the playhouse when he was young. He has endowed the restoration of the playhouse, which is listed on the National Register of Historic Places. You may wish to ask about the other buildings on the grounds that are scheduled for restoration.

Religious Sites

Annunciation Greek Orthodox Church
9400 West Congress Street (461-9400).
Three blocks north of Capitol Drive at 92nd Street.

- Open Monday-Friday 9am-2:30pm for group tours of 15 or more; smaller groups may be accommodated within larger ones; all tours must be arranged in advance.
- Admission, donation.

This blue-domed church was described by architect Frank Lloyd Wright as his "little jewel." It was Wright's last major project. The design of the building directs your focus upward. Architecturally, it's fascinating — the ceiling rests on ball bearings to expand and contract with Milwaukee's weather.

For a summer treat, combine your tour of the church with the Greek Festival on the weekend after the Fourth of July. We think it's one of the best church fairs in Milwaukee. See "Greek Festival" in Chapter 5.

▶ Special feature: If your tour group has 25 or more people, you may wish to enjoy a special luncheon treat; a Greek meal cooked by the members of the church. Reserve at least two weeks in advance.

Congregation Emanu-El B'ne Jeshurun Synagogue
2419 East Kenwood Boulevard (964-4100).
Across from the University of Wisconsin-Milwaukee Student Union.

- Open for tours Monday-Wednesday 9am-5pm; call in advance.
- Parking lot to the south of the building; use the Prospect Avenue entrance.
- Handicapped accessibility; use the parking lot entrance.

This Reform synagogue (1922) reflects the imposing style of Greek Revival architecture. The building is big, simple and lovely. The staff tour guides couldn't be nicer. They really are pleased to answer your questions; go ahead and ask them. The museum showcases are in the foyer. The 130-year-old Congregation welcomes visitors to the Sabbath worship services on Friday night and Saturday morning. Call for times.

Holy Hill-Carmelite Monastery

1525 Carmel Road, Hubertus 53033 (414/628-1838).
Highway 41 north from Milwaukee to state highway 167; west 7 miles.

- Information and reservations Monday-Friday 8am-4pm; religious services daily.
- Write or call to arrange group visits.
- Food service weekends year-round until 4pm; daily April 1-October 31; groups are requested to make meal arrangements in advance.
- Gift shop.
- Handicapped accessibility to church; call to make arrangements for special eating facilities.

The view from the scenic tower is especially beautiful in the fall and well worth the climb of 178 steps. Stop at the gift shop to obtain a pamphlet containing a self-conducted walking tour. Extend a leisurely fall weekend drive by picking apples in a local orchard; you'll see signs along the road. Dine at the Fox and Hounds Restaurant (1298 Friess Lake Road, 258-4100); Sunday brunch is particularly nice. While in the area, you may want to stop for some honey at Honey Acres (see Chapter 2).

St. Joan of Arc Chapel

Fourteenth Street at Wisconsin Avenue (224-6873).
In the heart of the Marquette University campus, not easily visible from the street.

- Open daily 10am-4pm; closed Thanksgiving, Christmas and New Year's Day; mass daily at noon, 4pm and 10pm except Saturday, Sunday 10am and noon.
- Admission, free.
- Public parking lot at Thirteenth and St. Paul streets.
- Handicapped accessibility through the Memorial Library only.

The medieval French family chapel was constructed in the fifteenth century near Lyon, France. It was reconstructed on the Marquette University campus in 1964. St. Joan of Arc is said to have worshipped in the chapel. Legend has it that the stone where she knelt to pray is colder than the surrounding stones. You're invited to see for yourself; put your hand on the stone. If you're still not convinced, there are charming docents to tell you more.

St. Josaphat's Basilica

2333 South Sixth Street (645-5623).
Exit I-94 at Beecher Street; 3 blocks west of the expressway.

- Open for religious services.
- Group tours following Sunday 10am mass; call Betty Panfil (321-3038) to arrange special tours; group tour admission, fee.
- Large parking lot to the south of the building.

This magnificent church was built at the turn of the century by immigrant parishioners and local craftsmen. With $20,000 of their hard-earned money, the parishioners purchased 500 railway flatcars of marble, limestone, granite columns, finished metal and woodwork salvaged from the demolished Chicago courthouse and post office. It's an unbelievable transformation! Look for the scales of justice on some of the doorknobs. A copper-clad dome and paintings on canvas adorn this beautiful church.

Included in "A Walk in the City: A Historical Walking Tour of Milwaukee's South Side" in Chapter 2.

2 Tour The Town

Commercial Tours

Planning a tour of the city? Your group may request a general tour or focus on a specific area of interest. Most of the tour companies with whom we spoke are happy to customize their tours to fit the needs of your group. Some provide mini-vans for small groups or handicapped needs. Just ask!

Archi-Tours
- Call for tour information (645-5300, 332-5019).

Milwaukee's three original settlements may be seen by bus. A comprehensive 1½ hour tour is available by appointment for groups.

Bravo Milwaukee
4212 West Highland Boulevard (344-4550 ext. 251).

A joint project of the Florentine Opera and the Milwaukee County Transit System. A multitude of tours from which to choose — gardens, pub crawls, breweries, sunset cruises, baseball, and even wine and cheese. Call for the complete tour packet. Program chairpersons will love these ideas. Reduced rates for senior citizens and youth groups on full daytime tours.

Gray Line
- For tour information, P.O. Box 977, Northbrook, Illinois 60062 (414/276-9588).
- Three-hour sight-seeing tours offered daily from Memorial Day to Labor Day.

Inner City Travel Company
2448 North Third Street (263-2727).
- Handicapped accessibility.
- Dinner/theatre tours to Chicago. Tours to the horse races at Arlington Park.

Milwaukee County Transit System Sight-Seeing Tours
4212 West Highland Boulevard (937-3251).
- Special summer tours June-August; regularly scheduled, no charter needed. Four pick-up locations in the Milwaukee area.
- Charter tours are available year-round.

Milwaukee Reflections
- Call for tour information (782-5087, 475-5912).

Schedule something special for your group! Hostesses Carol and JoAnn, dressed in elegant turn-of-the-century finery, will escort you into historic Milwaukee. Choose from four unique tours: tea on Yankee Hill, lunch at the Pabst Mansion, a Polish *zabawa* (amusement), or vintage churches citywide.

On the Scene with Eleanor Woods and Associates
6961 North Crestwood Drive 53209 (352-2840, 352-7626).

• Handicapped accessibility.

Tours of Milwaukee and Chicago tailored to your group's interests. Call or write for the complete brochure. Senior citizen discounts.

Tour About Inc.
For tour information, P.O. Box 1644, Racine, Wisconsin 53401 (414/632-8550).

Featuring the sites of southeastern Wisconsin including the Johnson Wax complex. Groups may be arranged or a guide will join your group.

Tours D'Art
2726 East Newberry Boulevard (964-8312).

• Handicapped accessibility may be arranged for small groups.

Art galleries, antique dealers, and artists' studios, some of which are not usually accessible, can be enjoyed on these tours. Try a trip to the Chicago Art Institute and some of the other Chicago art offerings. Complimentary refreshments.

University of Wisconsin-Extension/Department of History
For tour information, Miss Palmer, 114 MIT, UW-Milwaukee, P.O. Box 413, Milwaukee 53201 (963-5926).

Some of the past topics have included Frank Lloyd Wright, German Milwaukee, Women in Milwaukee, and the Genealogical Collection. Frequent trips are offered in spring, summer, and fall. Tours may be as short as half a day and as long as three days.

Boat Trips
Cruise and eat! Kids will like this too.

Emerald Isle Boat Line
Docks at 333 North Water Street (241-5631).

• Handicapped persons are easily accommodated.

Tours are offered daily April-September. Dinner cruises and Sunday brunch cruises available with seven days' notice and reservations. Full bar. Senior citizen discount.

Iroquois Boat Tour
Clybourn Street Bridge, downtown on the west side of the Milwaukee River (332-4194).

• Handicapped persons are easily accommodated.

Tours are offered 7 days a week mid-June–Labor Day. Senior citizen discounts. Snack bar. The cruises take you down the Milwaukee River and along the Lakefront. Allow about an hour and a half; special tours take a bit longer.

Driving and Walking Tours

Auto Tours

The following guide books are available for a small fee at the Department of City Development, 809 North Broadway Street (223-5796). These informative neighborhood guides contain easy-to-follow maps and tour routes.

See-For-Yourself Auto Tour For Home Seekers.
This tour is designed to acquaint you with Milwaukee's diverse neighborhoods. It is especially useful for newcomers who are searching for a home. This tour takes 10-12 hours, so plan rest stops at some of the area parks.

Discover Milwaukee: See For Yourself Auto Tours.
The flavor of every neighborhood is here, from Piggsville to Tippecanoe. The 13 booklets in this well-designed series explore in detail each residential area. They include maps, photographs, and historical information as well as interesting landmarks. The tours will take you through the full range of residential districts as well as some of the shopping areas and parks. Each tour lasts one hour. A must for newcomers who want to know what's what.

Walking Tours

When the weather cooperates, there is nothing more delightful than exploring Milwaukee's neighborhoods on foot. But if you're not a hearty hiker, or if you've got cabin fever on a −25° day, hop in your car; you don't *have* to walk to enjoy these tours. There are self-guided and guided tours available. We've provided a partial listing to get you started.

Wauwatosa Self-Guided Walking Tour

- Send 50¢ and a self-addressed stamped envelope to Wauwatosa Historical Society, 7611 Harwood Avenue, Wauwatosa, Wisconsin 53213.

This tour, one of our favorites featuring charming Victoriana, is particularly well laid out.

Waukesha Self-Guided Walking Tour

- Prepared by the Waukesha County Historical Society (414/548-7186).
- Pick up a map at 101 West Main Street.

Archi-Tours/Historic Milwaukee

- Call for informational brochure (332-5019, 645-5300).
- June 1-September 15, fee.

Your choice of tours: Yankee Hill, Kilbourntown (a lot of diversity here), Northpoint Watertower area, Walker's Point, and Juneautown (one of their best tours).

   Watch for other tours and times in the local newspapers. Allow one hour for touring.

University of Wisconsin-Extension/Department of History
- For information, Miss Palmer, 114 MIT, UW-Milwaukee, P.O. Box 413, Milwaukee 53201 (963-5926).

Walking tours highlighting local history are offered; allow about two hours for touring.

Northpoint Historical Society
- For listings and fees, P.O. Box 557, Milwaukee 53201.

Walking and bus tours are offered.

West Allis Walking Tour
- Guided walking tours; call for an appointment (321-3687).
- Self-guided walking tour brochure, send a self-addressed stamped envelope and 25¢ to West Allis Walking Tour, 8405 West National Avenue, West Allis 53227.

A Walk in the City

The three tours following were originally created by "Libraries for Milwaukee" under a grant from the National Endowment for the Humanities under the direction of the Library Council of Metropolitan Milwaukee.

A Historical Walking Tour of Milwaukee's South Side

Historical records show that until at least 1841 there was a Potawatomi Village at what is now Sixth Street and National Avenue. Forty years later the near South Side was a thriving community of German, Irish and Scandinavian immigrants and Yankees from the East. The community they built, known as Walker's Point, is the only one of the three original settlements which became Milwaukee in which a substantial percentage of the original buildings have survived.

Beginning in the 1870s large numbers of Polish immigrants began to settle in the area. They were thrifty and hardworking individuals who placed a high value on home ownership and willingly accepted the sacrifices necessary to save for land and the costs of building a house. Architectural historians refer to the typical mode of construction in this area as "additive." First, a family would build a simple house. Once it was paid for, the building was often underpinned or raised on bricks to create a walk-in basement apartment known locally as a "Polish flat." Many original homes were moved to the back of the lot so that new houses could be built. It is not uncommon in this area to see two or more structures on a single lot which have been converted into Polish flats.

Today this area continues to serve as a home for newcomers to the city. In the 1920s more than 100 Mexican workers were recruited by the Pfister & Vogel Tanning Co. This original group of settlers was soon joined by family members and they formed the core of Milwaukee's Spanish-speaking community, which continues to grow. The reasonably-priced housing in the area continues to attract numbers of people from rural areas as they move into the city.

The immigrants' mark on Milwaukee's cultural landscape is more readily evident in ordinary houses and shops than it is in formal "landmarks." This tour provides a brief introduction to both the conspicuous and the commonplace elements which make this South Side neighborhood unique.

1   Forest Home Library, 1432 W. Forest Home Ave.
Forest Home Library was built to consolidate the services of three other libraries — Lincoln, Layton Park, and South Side. The structure of steel, concrete, tinted glass and wood was built in 1966 under the direction of architects Van Grossman, Burroughs and Van Lanen. In 1967 the library received an honor award from the Wisconsin Chapter of the American Institute of Architects as "an alive and creative solution to small-scale public architecture."

2   Forest Home Avenue
Originally chartered in 1848 as the Janesville Plank Road, this route was a toll road serving farmers who brought their produce to city markets.

3 1824-26 S. 13th St.

This Cream City brick store and residence was built in 1892 by Theophil Dombrowski. Designed by architect Bernard Kolpacki, it features Italianate detailing in the bracketing and brickwork below the windows. The ornamented top of the pitched peak and the wrought iron railing appear to be prefabricated pieces that were applied by the contractor. The storefront area itself is quite large. The original windows were probably much taller than they are now, giving the building an especially bright appearance within. Like so many buildings of its era, it probably had wooden steps leading up to the doorway.

4   1924-24A S. 13th St.
A very typical building in this area, this Polish flat was built in 1890 as a single family home. Seventeen years later the original home was raised to accommodate a flat below. What appears to be the original front porch has been retained, giving the building an extra bit of character.

5   1949 S. 13th St.
In the late 1800s when Polish immigrants were building up this area, it was a prevailing practice to build two or more houses on the same lot. In this case the original building was built at the back of the lot and converted into a Polish flat in 1908. In 1915 the new house, which faces the street, was built. The most striking and unusual feature of this house is the two-story brick porch which sets it off from its more modest neighbors. Note the ornamental effect provided by the offset bricks, bay windows and columns.

6   1966 S. 13th St.
The Poles who built these houses tended to be financially conservative. If they borrowed to build their houses, it was a small amount for a short period of time. This house, built as a single-family unit in 1844, was underpinned in 1914 at a cost of only $300. Cement brick is a very common building material in this area. To avoid the common appearance of concrete it was fabricated to look like split stone and accentuated with a tooled mortar line.

7   2053 S. 13th St.
Another lovely Cream City brick building, this house features excellent woodwork and brick detailing, and interesting ironwork railings. Note how there appears to be a flower growing out of each corner of the railing. The unusual dormer in the roof is repeated on the south side to let a little extra light into the upper level. Beautiful stained glass windows are visible on the south side of the building.

8   2063 S. 13th St.
Although this 1891 brick building was built out of the same materials as its neighbor, the architect, Bernard Kolpacki, included some striking differences in design and detailing. The house was originally built essentially as it stands, and yet it closely resembles a Polish flat. It is interesting to note the subtle differences in the saw-toothed brick detailing on this house and on its neighbor at 2053 S. 13th St. Variations on this horizontal line of brick are visible throughout the area. The window treatment here is notable in the arched window and in the upper window with its narrow band of lights across the top. In both this house and the one at 2053 S. 13th St. we see an emphasis on letting in light that is quite unusual in an era of heavy front porches.

9   2101 S. 14th St.
Although commercial buildings stand on nearly every corner, there are a few that are especially intriguing. This tavern and flat was probably built in 1898. Like the Wiczynski Building at 1439 W. Becher St., the style is eclectic and definitely eye-catching.

10   St. Hyacinth's School and Hall, 2064 S. 14th St.
This parish hall building was designed by Bernard Kolpacki. It was built in 1891.

11   Convent of the School Sisters of Notre Dame, 2057 S. 14th St.
This building was designed by Henry Messmer, who also designed the parish's church and school. The six buildings of St. Hyacinth's form a harmonious ensemble based on consistency in the handling of scale, proportions and building materials.

12   St. Hyacinth's School, Becher St. at 14th St.

13   St. Hyacinth's Rectory, 1414 W. Becher St.
This rectory was built in 1886. It was the first of the three parish buildings designed by Bernard Kolpacki. The St. Hyacinth complex is given some sense of variety by the way architects Messmer and Kolpacki used both Gothic and Renaissance forms and details.

14   St. Hyacinth Church, 1414 W. Becher St.
Because of the rapid growth of the Polish community in the 1880s, a new parish was needed to supplement the resources of St. Stanislaus at Fifth and Mitchell. In 1882 the families west of 11th Street formed St. Hyacinth's parish and began construction of a new church. The building was designed by Milwaukee architect Henry Messmer, and is constructed of Cream City brick set on a limestone foundation. A richly modeled effect is achieved by the use of bays with brick pilasters and beautiful windows framed by stone and brick pedimented casings. Buff sandstone is used for the carved details and trim.

15   1437-39 W. Becher St.
This striking 1894 residential and commercial building is an excellent illustration of the "eclectic Milwaukee" style of architecture. There are two terra-cotta plaques, one with the building name and one in the peak of the gable. The saw-toothed brickwork repeats the pattern common to the neighborhood. The vase and coping in the broken pediment are made of pressed metal designed to resemble carved stone.

16   Kosciuszko Park, 721 W. Becher St.
Thaddeus Kosciuszko, a Polish hero of the American Revolution, is honored by this park which was originally part of the estate of a Universalist minister, Clement F. LeFeure. Although the appearance of the park and lagoon have been changed several times over the years, it remains an attractive and popular recreation spot. The most prominent monument is a striking statue of Kosciuszko on horseback by sculptor Gaetano Trentanove. Funds for the monument, which was installed in 1905, were raised by neighborhood residents. Construction is currently under way on a new recreational center on the site of the old boathouse. This multi-use 40,000 square-foot structure will include meeting rooms, a gymnasium and a library. When it is completed in the summer of 1982, the building will have special facilities on two levels to serve both teens and older adults.

17   St. Josaphat's Basilica, 2333 S. Sixth St.
To the southeast of the park the skyline is dominated by the copper-clad dome of St. Josaphat's Basilica, built in 1897-1901. Father Wilhelm Grutza, the pastor, salvaged the materials when the main post office building in Chicago was demolished. For $20,000 he purchased 500 railway flatcar loads of limestone, marble, polished granite columns, metalwork and woodwork. Milwaukee architect Erhard Brielmaier spent the next four years working with parishioners to build this imposing landmark. Work on the interior artwork continued until 1927. In 1929 the church was elevated to basilica status by Pope Pius XI.

18   South Stadium, Windlake and Becher Streets
When it was constructed in 1925, South Stadium, then known as City Stadium, was the first such high school facility in Milwaukee. Milwaukee's first House of Correction occupied this site from 1866 until the early 1900s when it was condemned as unsanitary. There was a 16-foot fence around the facility, and outside the fence were popular city baseball diamonds. If a player hit a hardball over the fence, he might bribe an inmate with a pack of cigarettes to get it back.

19   Kosciuszko Junior High School, 971 W. Windlake Ave.
This building was designed by a school administration architect, Guy E. Wiley. Construction began in December 1925, and the school opened in the fall of 1927. The original cost of this durable structure was $640,000.

20   954 W. Windlake Ave.
Here is an example of additive architecture resulting in an extremely interesting, if a bit chaotic, building. The house was originally built in 1884, the first addition in 1904. Finally, in 1919, the Polish flat was created. It is interesting to note that the house appears to be facing every possible cross street, even though its true front is on Windlake.

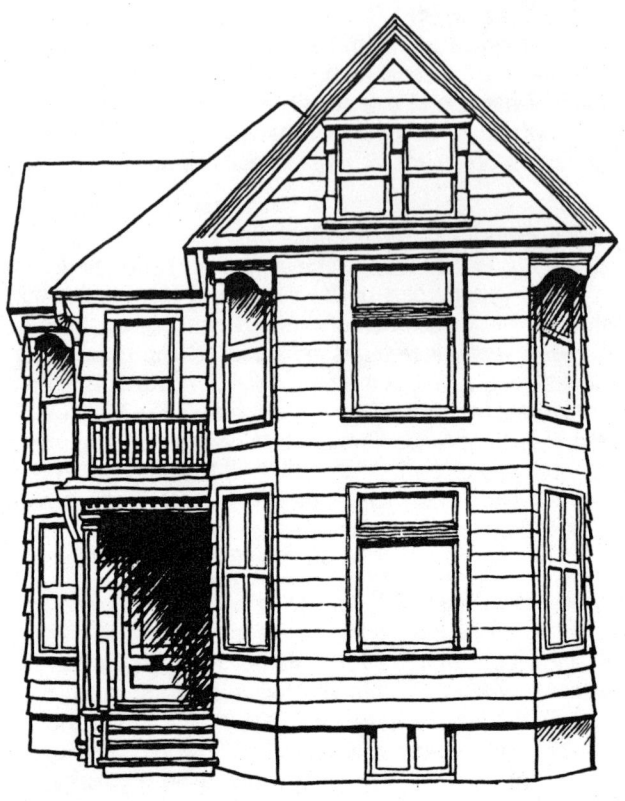

21   922 W. Windlake Ave.
Notice here the nicely cornered, diagonal windows, a detail that is seen several times in this neighborhood. The carpenter has used brackets to hold the roof up over the corner windows. Built in 1884 and under-pinned in 1909, the house has a very unusual roof line with a parallel "double valley" effect.

22   854 W. Windlake Ave.
The original appearance of this 1905 residence and tavern is a bit difficult to reconstruct, but there is evidence of some unusual window treatments. Notice the outward curving lines above the door. Along Ninth Street three below-grade windows with arched lintels once let in light on the lower level.

23   836-38 W. Maple St.
This old wood frame building was built as a barbershop in 1892. It stands out because of its size and simple styling. In the late 1950s the structure was converted from commercial use to a three-family residence.

24   St. Anthony's Catholic Church, 1705 S. 9th St.
Although it was originally built to serve a German-speaking congregation, St. Anthony's subsequently came to serve the area's Polish residents. This Gothic Revival church was designed by Naescher and Heer of Dubuque, Iowa. Work on this lovely building was begun in 1877 and completed nine years later.

25   St. Stanislaus Catholic Church, 1669 S. Fifth St.
Looking east from the corner of Ninth and Mitchell, one has a view of St. Stanislaus Church, the third Polish parish to be established in the United States. This Milwaukee landmark was designed by architect Leonard Schmidtner. Both the exterior and the interior of the German-styled, late-Renaissance structure have been altered several times. The most recent renovation project, designed by Milwaukee architect Mark A. Pfaller, included replacing the original copper-clad cupolas with gold-plated domes. Completion of the renovation coincided with the parish centennial in 1966.

26   Mitchell Street
In the 1880s Mitchell Street was already a budding commercial street. In April 1920, the Milwaukee Electric Railway and Light Co. established an innovative motorbus route along Mitchell Street, enhancing its growth as a commercial district, and by the 1930s it had become the "Polish Grand Avenue," offering major stores, financial institutions and theaters to serve the community. Extensive renovation of Mitchell Street — from Fifth to 15th streets — was completed during the 1970s.

27   929 W. Mitchell St.
This attractive office building with its stone-rope decoration was designed by architects Gurda and Gurda. Built at a cost of $55,000 in 1924, it shows that Mitchell Street was a thriving commercial area in that decade.

28   931 W. Mitchell St.
This building and the one at 929 W. Mitchell St. are joined and share a common doorway, even though the styles of the two buildings are quite different.

29   1039-41 W. Mitchell St.
The Mitchell Street State Bank has just been renovated and remodeled by its owners. It was built in 1916 at a cost of $40,000.

30   Modjeska Theater, 1134 W. Mitchell St.
In the 1920s there were six theaters on Mitchell Street. The most important of these was built in 1911 and named the Modjeska after the Polish actress Madame Helena Modjeska. It was rebuilt in 1924 to become the second largest theater in the state with a stage show, vaudeville acts, a theater organ and its own orchestra.

31   Farmers Market, 1321 W. Mitchell St.
This was the site of St. Jacobi's Evangelical Lutheran Church. The church was originally dedicated in 1873 to serve Lutherans who had emigrated from Germany, and continued to offer German-language services until 1971. In 1906 a new church was dedicated. It was an imposing red brick and masonry building with large stained glass windows. Twin spires 62 feet high crowned the landmark. Over the next few decades the families of the congregation moved out of the area and the church purchased land on 86th Street and Forest Home Avenue to build still another church and school. The old church was finally demolished in 1977. Many Milwaukee residents still lament the loss of this lovely Gothic structure. Today the land is used as a farmers market built in conjunction with the Mitchell Center street renovation.

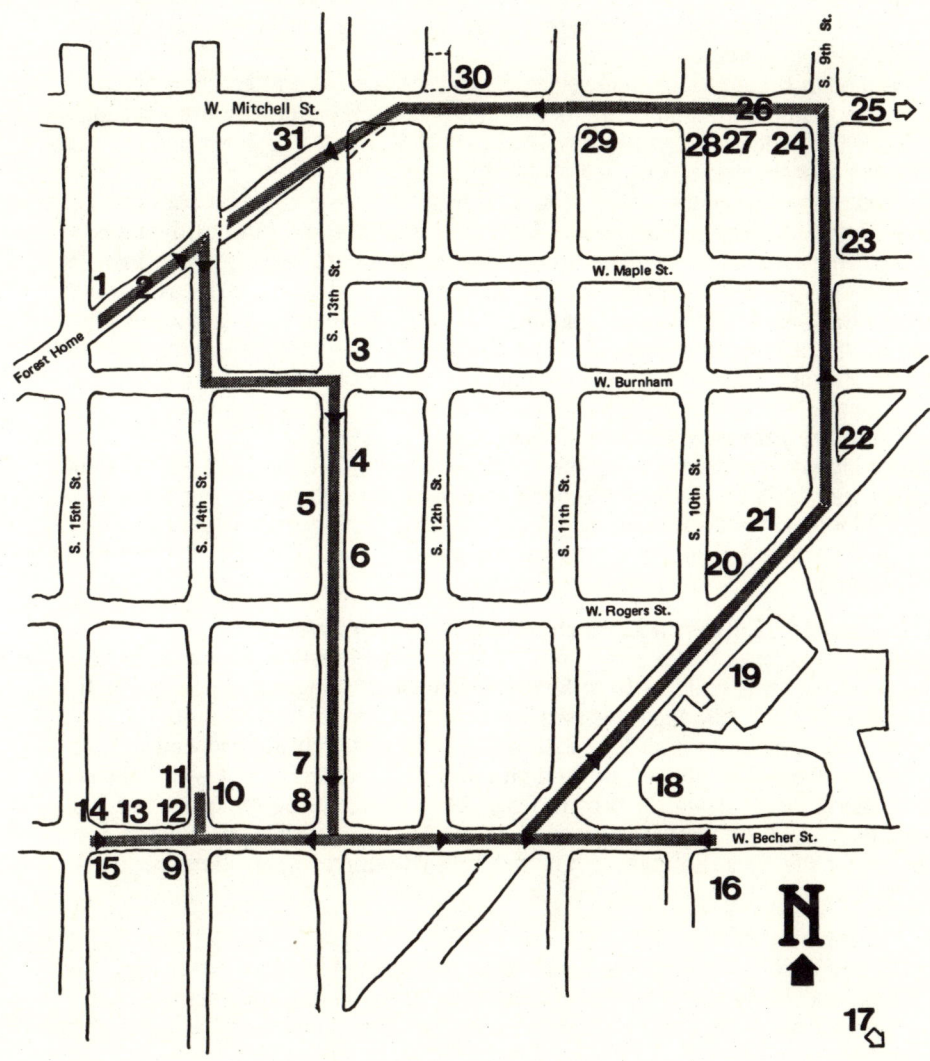

A Historical Walking Tour of Milwaukee's West Side

Other than an occasional farmhouse, there was little development on the upper West Side of Milwaukee until the turn of the 20th century. During the first 20 years of this century, row after row of sturdy homes were built, primarily by second-generation Americans who had moved west from their North Side neighborhoods. Although there were a few wealthy families like the Harleys and Davidsons, the majority of those who settled in the area were middle-class merchants or professionals.

Although the area's original settlers were for the most part children of German-speaking immigrants, the bungalows and duplexes now house residents from a wide variety of backgrounds. This part of Milwaukee features one of the city's highest concentrations of well-preserved older homes.

Today the face of the upper West Side bears the scars of urban planning gone awry. Despite widespread opposition from area residents and businessmen, 983 houses were torn down to make way for the ill-fated Park West freeway. In 1979 the freeway was officially removed from county planning maps, a decision which opened the way for renewed development of this three-mile-long strip of empty land in the heart of the West Side. The outcome of the current planning process will be an important factor in the evolution of the whole area.

1   Finney Library, 4243 W. North Ave.

Finney Library has been serving the public since July 6, 1953. Built for $228,000 Finney was the first new neighborhood library constructed by the city since 1913. Grassold-Johnson Associates designed the building. During remodeling in 1979, the firm Architecture 360 included a skylighted planter as a key design element in the new addition.

2   Parkside Lutheran Church, 4311 W. North Ave.

In 1938, 19 families broke away from St. Matthew's Church at 10th and Garfield and purchased this building from Sherman Boulevard Congregational Church. The price was $38,000, although assessed valuation was closer to $200,000. The church was remodeled and dedicated as a Lutheran church in October 1939. Originally there was a tower on the north end of the building, but with heavier traffic along the boulevard it began to crumble and had to be removed. For 10 years Parkside's congregation shared the building with Emmanuel Lutheran Church for the Deaf. Emmanuel now has its own church across the street on North Avenue.

3   Sherman Boulevard

At the suggestion of Milwaukee's early park commissioners, 43rd Street was widened and made into a boulevard between Perrigo Park (now Sherman) and West Park (now Washington). Over the years Sherman Boulevard has been altered several times as a result of increasing traffic, but a considerable number of beautiful and well-maintained examples of late 19th- and early 20th-century architecture survive in the blocks between the parks. Early residents of Sherman Boulevard recall the farmers' fields behind the houses on the west side of the street.

4   2203-05 N. Sherman Blvd.
Architect Henry Rotier designed this imposing home for a local manufacturer in 1911. The use of heavy timber and rough stucco reflects a 20th century revival of interest in European style buildings of the Medieval Period. Notice the lovely woodwork on the glass-enclosed porch and the half-timber beam construction of the attic.

**5   Monument to Baron Friedrich Wilhelm Von Steuben,
    at the intersection of Sherman Blvd., Lisbon Ave. and Lloyd St.**
This statue of the Revolutionary War hero Von Steuben, was a gift of the Huehlenberg Unit of the Von Steuben Society, a German-American cultural organization. The equestrian statue was unveiled in a ceremony of July 3, 1921. Von Steuben was an aide to General George Washington and an Inspector General of the American Army.

6   Lisbon Avenue
Lisbon Avenue was a transportation route long before the Milwaukee street patterns were developed. Originally called the Lisbon Plank Road, the route was traveled by farmers from Butler and other outlying agricultural areas who brought their goods to Milwaukee. Its status as a commercial street was later enhanced by a streetcar line and its proximity to Washington Park.

7   Washington Park, 4020 W. Vliet St.
In the *History of Milwaukee County,* published in 1895, Howard Lewis Conard describes West (now Washington) Park as "a superb piece of undulating or even hilly land of one hundred and twenty-four and fifty-one hundredths acres in extent. It is likewise the highest point of land surrounding the city... From this point there is a superb view of the whole city and the Bay of Milwaukee, as well as the lovely and well-timbered hillocks toward the west."

Washington Park has always been a favorite gathering place for West Side families who came to enjoy a wide range of outdoor activities. Most Milwaukeeans remember Washington Park Zoological Gardens, which were created in 1908 and remained until 1958. And, of course, it was not summer in Milwaukee without band concerts at Washington Park.

Early in the 20th century one of Washington Park's biggest attractions was a harness racing track along Lisbon Avenue, between 40th Street and Sherman Boulevard. In the middle of the track were baseball diamonds, which were also tremendously popular. Older residents of the area recall having to wait for the horses to pass before they could get across to the ball fields. Although the race track is now gone, baseball diamonds still exist at the site.

Although the "well-timbered hillocks" were long ago reshaped by the developer's axe, Washington Park has continued to be a year-round recreational haven for the West Side. More recent attractions include the Emil Blatz Temple of Music (more commonly known as "the bandshell") which was built in 1938, the Washington Park Senior Center, and the new solar heated boathouse.

8   3940 W. Lisbon Ave.
Built in 1925 at a cost of $78,000, this 24-family apartment building reflects the increasing population density of the area in the '20s. Although the style of the building is essentially modern, the lovely curved corner is quite old-fashioned. The arch above the door, the light and graceful colonnade between the five windows, and the garlanded panel between the second and third stories add character to the building, as do the leaded glass windows.

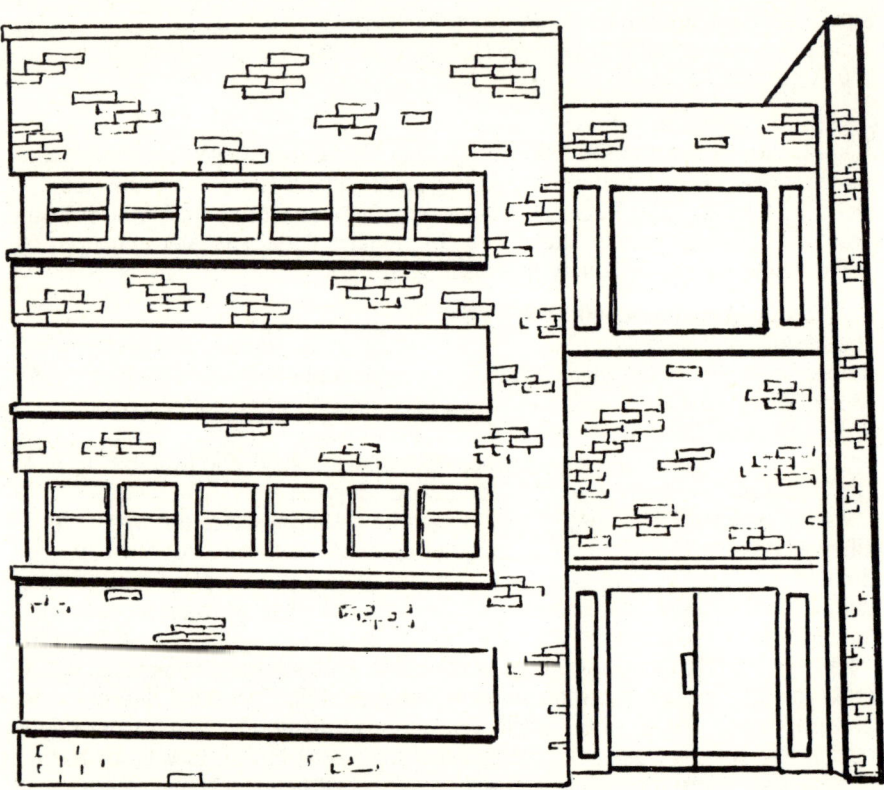

9   4018 W. Lisbon Ave.
A fundamentally modern building with brick panels wrapping around it and with rows of small windows, this commercial structure is reminiscent of a modern European style in architecture.

10   Club 41, 4104 W. Lisbon Ave.
This is an interesting attempt at modernizing the facade of an older commercial building to make it more eye-catching. Notice the way the horizontal stripes turn around the corner.

11   2023-25 N. 41st St.
Although the area is full of duplexes, this one offers a fresh approach. It appears to be a cross between a duplex and a double house. In recent years the two units have been converted for use as a rooming house.

12   2037 N. 41st St.
This house, built in 1909 by carpenter George Mommel, is a typical workingman's "story-and-a-half." Because the roof begins halfway up the second story, upstairs bedrooms or the attic have angled ceilings along the outer edges.

13   2038-40 N. 41st St.
One of the earlier houses on the block, this sturdy duplex was built in 1905 and reflects some of the architectural attitudes of the day. The building is constructed of an early version of concrete block cut to resemble stone. On the more hidden south side of the building the concrete is left perfectly plain, indicating a feeling that although concrete may be an ideal building material, it is too vulgar for the "public" sides of a structure. Another interesting feature is what appears to be a converted stable on Garfield Avenue. Perhaps the original owner thought that the automobile was a passing fancy.

14   2103-05 N. 40th St.
Contractor Henry Hunholz built a number of the houses on the block, all of which feature a distinctive bit of detailing in the eaves. The houses are not designed in any particular style, but rather incorporate features of several different styles. The result could be called the "Hunholz style."

15   2120-22-22A N. 40th St.
Because it is built on a double lot, this house stands out from its neighbors. Built in 1903, it was very likely one of the first houses on the block, and may have set the style for the neighborhood. Many of the features recur throughout the area. Notice the carpentry work on the false capitals at the top of the porch columns. These appear to be cartouches — decorative ornaments grouped around the tops of the columns. Notice also the Palladian window in the gable. This is an arched central window with a smaller window on each side, typical of the Classical Revival style in architecture. Another interesting feature is the arched treatment of the porch railing.

16   2123-25 N. 40th St.
This is another typical building for this area, especially in the neighborhood west of Sherman Boulevard. Watch for the double columns supporting the porch roof, a detail which recurs throughout the area. Another popular architectural technique is the emphasis on the second story sill line rather than on the actual story line. This gives the upper portion of the building a lighter, more graceful feeling than is evident on the first floor.

17   2146 N. 40th St.
Built in 1905, this is a narrow version of a typical American "farmhouse" style building. Two common Milwaukee features are the very high pitch of the roof and the thickness of the gable treatment. Compare the edges of this roof to those on the gambrel-style roof at 2144 N. 40th St., which is more typical of the roof treatment used in other parts of the country.

18   2153 N. 40th St.
The fine carpentry work on the porch gives a very distinctive look to this house. Note the variety of porch railings on what are essentially similar houses in this area. In this case there is a variety of railings on one house.

19   2152-54 N. 40th St.
This duplex was built in 1919 by Henry Hunholz, who also built several of the nearby homes. The applied woodwork in a plant form on the gable is typical of the practice of using mass-produced architectural details to give a touch of individuality to very similar structures. Notice that the same plant form appears in miniature at 2156 N. 40th St., built by Hunholz in 1909.

20   2163-65 N. 40th St.
The stucco and the hexagonal roofing shingles used on this duplex were both highly popular just after the turn of the century. This 1909 house, designed by Charles W. Valentine, has been given a somewhat medieval look through the use of heavy timber work. Notice the heavy proportions of the porch and the small angular braces over the main entrance. The small, thin window on the front gable of the attic area is typical of the late Tudor Revival style. This style is more often seen in much larger houses on the East Side.

21   2170-72 N. 40th St.
This home, built in 1919 by Henry Hunholz, has a Classical Revival feeling created by the Ionic columns of the front porch and the fancy millwork detail in the front gable. The consoles hanging down from the little gable in the attic are actually classical volutes turned upside down by the carpenter and used in an atypical way that has nothing at all to do with classical architecture. The metal porch railing is a Hunholz trademark which appears on three of his houses on this street.

22   2175-77 N. 40th St.
The influence of Frank Lloyd Wright and the Chicago School of architects is evident in the proportions of this building constructed in 1912. The influence is especially seen in the highlighting of horizontal features. Notice the use of strip windows and the story course at the top of the brickwork that includes the roof and front porch. The differentiation of shingles above and the other materials below is very common in the neighborhood.

23   Christian Union Baptist Church, 2176 N. 39th St.
Built in 1913 as Washington Park Presbyterian Church, this building has been remodeled several times. It displays traits of neo-Northern Renaissance style architecture; the ornamental gables give it a Spanish or Dutch Baroque feeling. At the rear entrance, on Garfield Avenue, the roof projects over the vestibule at an angle that matches the angle of the roof above. The three windows tucked under the eave of the roof are a sensitive detail above the doorway.

24   3830 W. Garfield Ave.
This is another instance of the influence of the Prairie School of architects. It is similar to the house at 2175-77 N. 40th St., but on a more humble scale. Here the roof line and strip windows reflect the Prairie School, but the bay windows do not. Bay windows are, however, very common in this neighborhood and serve to link this 1912 house with its neighbors.

25   2212 N. 39th St.
This white clapboard house stands out for the symmetry of its design. It was built in 1908, one of the early homes in the neighborhood. The large glass-enclosed porch, three dormers, and proportioned hedges add to its country style.

26   North Avenue
North Avenue evolved as the primary business district for the neighborhood, reaching its peak development in the 1920s. Although the popularity of the shopping district has declined, the many fine commercial buildings still retain some of the flavor of the years of growth. The avenue was developed as a commercial strip, with residences above nearly all of the storefronts. The idea of combining residential and commercial uses has been popular throughout Milwaukee.

27   3901-03 W. North Ave.
This modern-looking commercial building was built in 1929 to house two stores and eight apartments. It replaced a store and dwelling that had been on the site since 1907. The striking feature of the building is the use of bas-relief panels for decoration.

28   4001 W. North Ave.
Each of Milwaukee's major breweries built taverns in its own distinctive style. This building was built in 1909 by the Miller brewery. The Northern Italianate style structure was designed to fit into this street corner.

29   Park West Freeway land
It is possible to see the Park West Corridor from North Avenue by looking north along any of the north-south cross streets. This strip of land was originally cleared to make way for the freeway which now will not be built. The "corridor" runs east three miles from Sherman Boulevard.

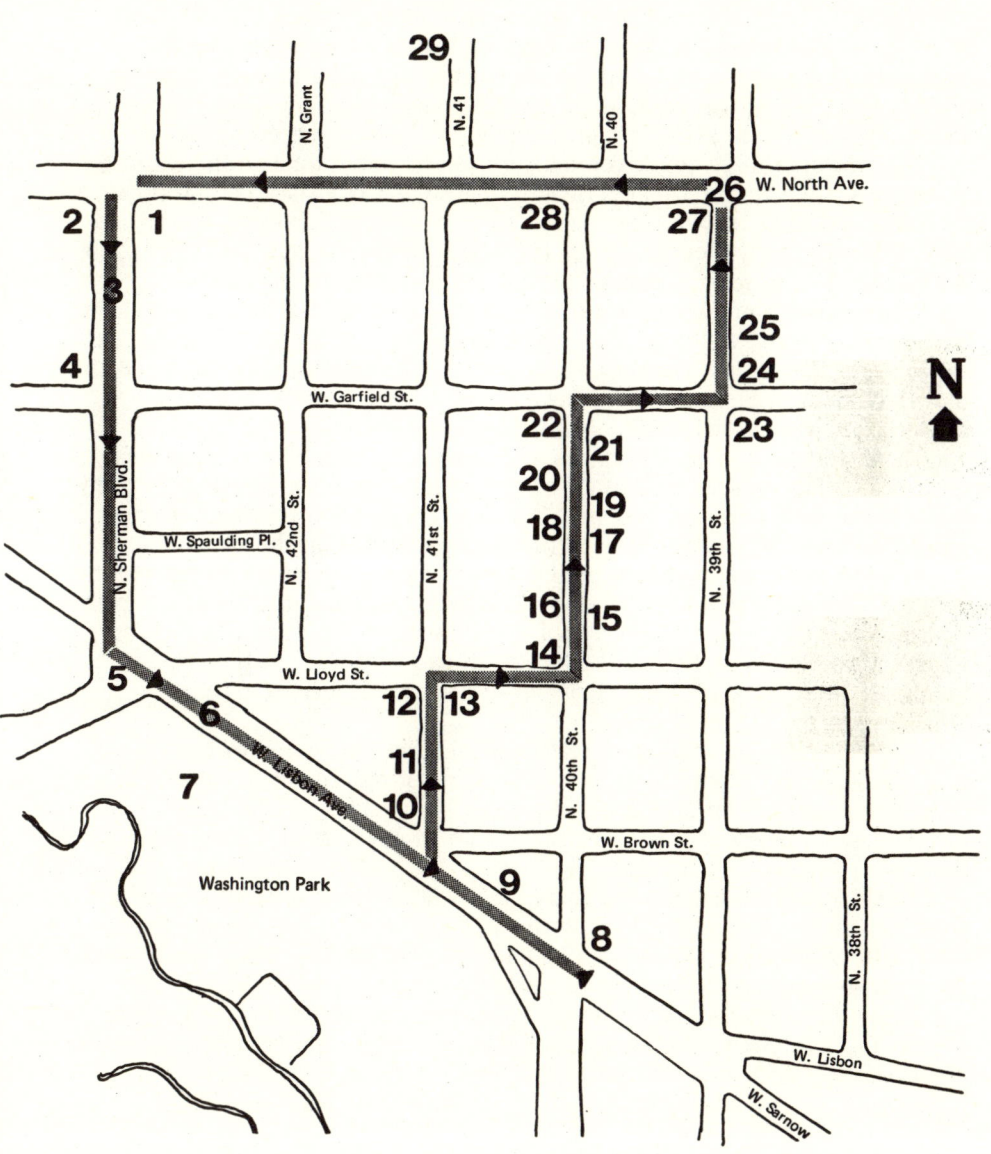

A Historical Walking Tour of Milwaukee's East Side

Milwaukee's East Side is really several neighborhoods, each with a fascinating history of changes from generation to generation. The area of this tour, which is just south of North Avenue and east of the Milwaukee River, is especially interesting because of the distinctly different communities which developed here.

The 1870s were a time of rapid expansion of industry along the Milwaukee River. Railroad development, tanneries and ice houses were magnets for immigrant families seeking work and the opportunity to build a home in their new land. At first these settlers were primarily Polish and Irish. They were hardworking and thrifty people who placed a high value on land and home ownership.

The growth of these ethnic communities can be traced through the churches created to serve them. In 1871 St. Hedwig's parish was established at the corner of Humboldt and Brady where it provided a focus of activity for the rapidly expanding Polish community. Fourteen years later, Holy Rosary Church was built at 2000 N. Oakland Ave. to serve a smaller but thriving Irish settlement there.

As the Polish community swelled in numbers it spread northward along Humboldt Avenue on the west side of the Milwaukee River. To accommodate this expansion new Polish churches were established. In 1893, St. Casimir was founded at 2618 N. Bremen St. and in 1907 yet another Polish parish, St. Mary's of Czestochowa, was created at 3055 N. Fratney St.

There were no zoning laws before 1920, so people were free to build their cottages and flats with an eye to making the most out of expensive land. In many cases houses were built and later modified to add walk-down basement quarters. It was not unusual for a family to build two or more houses on the same lot.

In the 1920s many members of Milwaukee's Italian community began moving from the "Old Third Ward" to the lower East Side. In 1925 Our Lady of Pompeii Church, which served the Third Ward Italians, established a mission church at 1329 N. Cass St. and in 1938 St. Rita's Church was completed at 1601 N. Cass St. In this period a distinctive Italian influence became evident in shops and restaurants in the Brady Street area.

In the decades following the Great Depression the Polish and Irish communities began to dwindle as older residents died or moved out of the area to settle in newer and less crowded parts of the city. As members of the Italian community grew in prosperity they also moved into newer areas of the city and suburbs.

By the 1960s the inexpensive flats in the neighborhood attracted a steadily growing number of younger people to the area and Brady Street became the acknowledged center of Milwaukee's youth or "hippie" culture. Many ethnic shops gave way to merchants selling records, blue jeans and jewelry.

Today the lower East Side retains characteristics of each of the groups that has lived or lives there. The architectural offerings range from vernacular cottages of the 1880s to once-proud mansions on Farwell Avenue; from "Polish flats" to high-rises; from simple storefronts to the opulent Oriental Theatre.

1   East Library, 1910 E. North Ave.
A number of esthetic features of East Library are notable, including the metal screen space divider, designed by Milwaukee artist Guido Brink; the decorative slab glass panels, designed and executed by Conrad Schmitt Studios; and the collection of 14 paintings by Wisconsin artists, donated by Mr. and Mrs. William D. Vogel. The library itself was designed by architects Darby, Bogner and Associates, and was opened to the public in November 1968. Since that time, it has been a focal point for East Side community activity.

2   East North Ave.
Throughout its history, this bustling street has served as a transfer point for trains, streetcar lines and buses. Beginning in 1886, a Cream City Railroad line and the Whitefish Bay Railroad Company's "dummy" line intersected at North and Farwell avenues. The small steam "dummy" trains carried Milwaukeeans northward along Farwell and Downer avenues to the popular Whitefish Bay resort area. The Cream City Railroad served the downtown area. Streetcar Route 21 began running west along North Avenue from Farwell in 1897. In 1933, a new terminal was built at Murray and North avenues to serve the line. Although city maps indicate that there was a bridge linking the east and west sides of North Avenue in 1880, the North Avenue Bridge as we know it was not completed until 1921.

3   2032 N. Cambridge Ave.
In the late 19th century, when this part of the city was bring rapidly built up, the "additive" mode of architecture was very common in ethnic neighborhoods. First, a small house was built and, once it was paid for, the owner added new rooms. This example of the additive style was built in 1890. In 1892 the roof was raised to make a place for two new rooms. The detailing along the eaves and porch is common in the area. They were purchased ready-made from catalogs rather than crafted by the builder.

4   2028 N. Cambridge Ave.
Although the original appearance of this 1890 house has been considerably altered by the addition of aluminum siding, some of its original Italianate features are still evident. Notice the long, thin windows and the bracketing along the eaves.

5   Caesar's Park, N. Warren Ave. at E. Boylston St.
This park, which was named after neighborhood resident Caesar Paikowski, overlooks the Milwaukee River and offers an excellent view of the Polish settlement west of the river. In 1883 the Humboldt Street Bridge was constructed, and the Polish community began to move northward along Humboldt Avenue. The River West neighborhood, which is visible here, offers many of the same features as this neighborhood, notably the "Polish flats" and back cottages.

6   1920 N. Warren Ave.
Queen Anne style cottages like this one are popular in this neighborhood. The house was built in 1890 and, like many of the houses in the area, it has been occupied by the same family for many years. Behind the house a typical back cottage is visible.

7   1906-08 N. Warren Ave.
This house, built in 1900, reflects an eclectic style that might be described as Queen Anne aspiring to Gothic. The grouping of various types of details is unique. Notice the double brackets on each side of the bay and the Gothic brackets and arch in the front bay. The windows in the cupola are Queen Anne, but the windows in the eaves are in the Gothic style. The porch is an example of Classical Revival style, which was very popular at the turn of the century. Note, too, the original ironwork and cresting above the windows.

8   1900-02 N. Warren Ave.
The Polish people who settled in this area tended to move and to re-use buildings rather than tear them down. When St. Hedwig's parish built its new rectory on Humboldt Avenue, the old house was sold and moved to this site. This brick structure is a good example of the Queen Anne features which are common in the neighborhood.

9   1860-62 N. Arlington Pl.
The detailing on the lintels and the grouping of three windows identify this 1885 cottage as early Italianate in style. The original structure was raised to accommodate a "Polish flat." It is interesting to notice that the builder imitated the original elongated windows in the design of the later and lower level.

10   1819-21 N. Arlington Pl.
This turn-of-the-century structure is an interesting example of both the additive style, and the combining of residential and commercial uses which was possible before the introduction of zoning laws.

11   1812-14 N. Arlington Pl.
In 1894 the original building on this site was raised in order to add a brick basement and, a few years later, the structure was altered to create a store in front and a two-story flat in the rear. Over the years the building has housed a grocery store, a macaroni business, a gift and novelty shop, a soap company, and a shoe repair shop. It was altered once more in the 1970s for use as the Eastside Artists' Cooperative. Now the building has returned to purely residential use.

12   Pulaski Street
When Polish settlers began arriving in this area in the late 1800s, they found that much of the high ground had already been settled by the Yankees and Irish. They were able to use an abandoned field, marked by a deep ravine which they partially filled and renamed *Ulicia Pulaskego* or Pulaski Street. This narrow, crooked street retains a turn-of-the-century flavor with its closely packed cottages and "Polish flats."

13   1729-31 N. Pulaski St.
The building was built in 1898 as a livery stable, as evidenced by the second floor hayloft doors and hook. In 1905 the Suminski Funeral Home, now at 1720 E. Brady St., took over the building. Today this is the home of the Peters-Werland Organ Company.

14   1760 N. Franklin Pl.
This small Queen Anne cottage, built in 1875, is a good example of the lower, pitched roofs of older buildings. As the construction trades grew more skilled, the roofs were built steeper. Compare the slope of this roof to the one across the street at 1138-40 E. Hamilton St.

15   1728-30 N. Franklin Pl.
Milwaukee architect Bernard Kolpacki used brick detailing to define the arch of the original window in this 1891 store and residence. Kolpacki also designed a number of Cream City brick buildings on the South Side, including the rectory and the hall for St. Hyacinth's Parish at 14th and Becher streets.

16   1729 N. Franklin Pl.
John Laczepanski built this flat in 1894 for $1,000 by re-using materials from another building that had been torn down. Like so many lots in this area, this property has two houses on it. Note that both the front and back houses were subsequently underbuilt to create "Polish flats." The unusually large front porch was added to this Queen Anne vernacular structure in 1921.

17   St. Hedwig's Catholic Church, Humboldt Avenue and Brady Street
Many of the early Polish settlers in this area were actually natives of the Kaszuby region on Poland's Baltic coast. Most of the "Kaszubs" settled on Jones Island, where they worked as fishermen, but some were attracted by the tanneries and ice houses along the Milwaukee River. St. Hedwig's parish grew rapidly. In the fall of 1871 there were 40 families. Three years later there were 250 families in the parish and it was still growing. Before St. Hedwig's was built, the East Side Poles had to walk all the way to St. Stanislaus on the South Side to hear a Polish language Mass. The working-class parishioners' devotion to St. Hedwig's is evident in the complex of buildings — church, school, rectory and convent — in what is now the heart of a very crowded neighborhood. The builders displayed the same thrift and ingenuity that is evident in their use of residential and commercial land. At various times in its history the parish outgrew its buildings or felt the need for new structures. Rather than tearing down old buildings, they were sold off and moved to new locations.

18   1701 N. Arlington Pl.
This building is an ideal example of the recycling of outgrown buildings. The structure was originally the St. Hedwig's Parish School. In 1875, when a larger school was needed, the parish raffled off this building for $1 per ticket. The winner, Francis Miszewski, subsequently sold it for $50 to Joseph Polcznski, who moved it from the St. Hedwig's complex on Humboldt and Brady to its present location.

19   Brady Street
A walk down Brady Street is always a feast for the senses. Behind 1870s wooden storefronts there is a remarkable variety of 1980s businesses, primarily ethnic shops and off-beat boutiques. In summer the air is often filled with rock music, and delicious smells drift from the restaurants and shops along the street.

20   1420 E. Brady St.
Although it has been extensively damaged by fire and neglect, this combination commercial and residential building is still a nice example of a Cream City brick apartment building. The Queen Anne structure was designed by Marshall and Ryder and built in 1895 at a cost of $21,000. (Subsequently demolished — eds.)

21   1708 N. Farwell Ave.
This building and the one at 1714 N. Farwell Ave. are typical East Side houses. The style is a combination of Queen Anne and Gothic revival. The Queen Anne hooded windows in the eaves, however, are unusual. This 1890 building is a reminder that both Prospect and Farwell avenues were once lined with substantial mansions.

22   1511 E. Royall Pl.
Milwaukee architect Walter A. Holbrook designed this Queen Anne style house. It was built in 1891 at a cost of $8,000. The structure, with its distinctive tower, stands in sharp contrast to the houses to the west, which are also in the Queen Anne style. The siding, which was added in 1944, covers very narrow boards and greatly alters the original proportions of the building.

23   1502-04 E. Royall Pl.
This double house was designed by architect Charles Kirchoff. It was built in 1881 at a cost of $6,200.

24   1823 and 1825 N. Oakland Ave.
These nearly identical houses present an interesting example of how changes in siding surfaces can alter the whole feel of a building. When siding is added for economy and ease of maintenance, it is all too tempting to remove architectural details rather than to work around them. That is what appears to have happened at 1823 N. Oakland Ave.

25   1923-25 N. Oakland Ave.
This elegant duplex in the Classical Revival style is much more like the larger houses along Prospect Avenue than its immediate neighbors. This structure was built in 1896 at a cost of $7,000. The design, by architect Charles Fitzgerald, is noteworthy for its attractive window treatment.

26   1973-75-77-79 N. Oakland Ave.
This fourplex was designed by architect H.H. Betts and built in 1896 at a cost of $6,600. The southern European influences on the Classical Revival style are in evidence here. The window in the eastern eave is in the style called "Palladian," after the Renaissance architect Andrea Palladio. The large geometric massing of this structure and the Greek columns on the front porch are characteristic of the Classical Revival style.

27   Holy Rosary Catholic Church, 2000 N. Oakland Ave.
St. John's Cathedral was the only English language Roman Catholic Church on the city's East Side until 1884. The decision was then made to establish Holy Rosary Parish to serve the English-speaking population north of Albion Street. Father McGill was appointed pastor and in 1885 the cornerstone for the new parish was laid. In October of that year the Sisters of Charity, B.V.M. opened the first parish school in the convent. Enrollments grew quickly; and in 1893 the school building was constructed. From the beginning Holy Rosary was identified as the "Irish church" while St. Hedwig's was considered the parish of the Poles. Although these labels persist today, both congregations draw parishioners from a variety of ethnic backgrounds, including Irish, Polish, German and Italian.

28   1718-36 E. Lafayette Pl.
The outstanding features of this Classical Revival row house are the many bays and dormers and the gambrel-roofed Flemish gable. The use of shake or shingles in the gables is a common feature of row houses in this area. It is interesting to notice that the bricks used on the front of the building are of higher quality and are laid more tightly together than those on the sides.

29 Oriental Landmark Theatre, 2230 N. Farwell Ave.
Between 1915 and 1930, movie palaces like this one were the favorite escape from day-to-day routines. The Oriental is a fine example of a period movie house. Movie palaces were often built in the most flamboyant and foreign styles possible. The Oriental's architects, Gustav Dick and Alex Bauer, created a theatre based on exotic oriental themes and popular motifs. Their complex conception is readily seen in the green, onion-shaped domes and in the terra-cotta lions, Buddha-graced balconies, murals, and silverleaf elephants of the interior. The Oriental was located here because it was at the end of a trolley line from the center of the city. The lower portion of the building was remodeled in 1957.

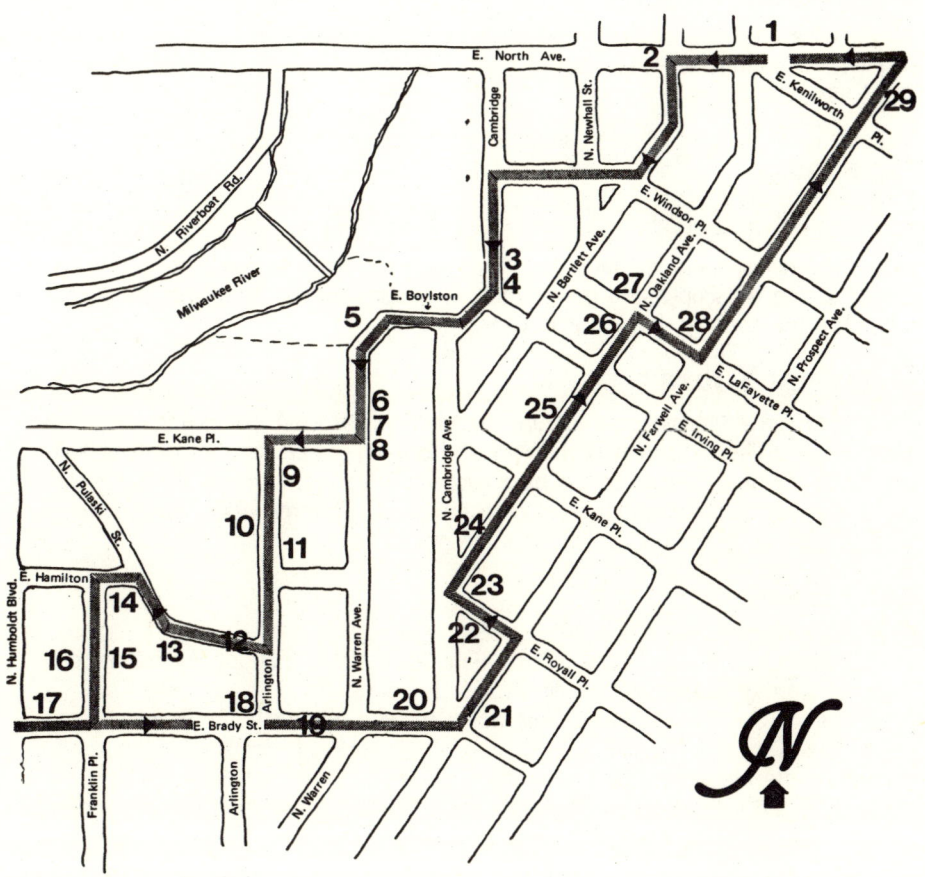

Behind the Scenes

Astronomical Society Observatory—Milwaukee County

18850 West Observatory Road (785-0926 evenings, 352-7144).
I-94 west to Moreland Road; south to National Avenue; west 1 mile to Observatory Road; north 2 miles.

- Group tours by appointment; summer open houses are scheduled May-September.
- Admission, free.
- Parking on the grounds.

Watch the newspapers for dates and times of open houses. You'll be able to use the 12½-inch telescopes and the 26-inch telescope, one of the largest amateur-owned in the country. Inquire about membership.

Brewery Tours

Come and see a Milwaukee tradition: the malting, brewing, packaging, and shipping of beer. There's a treat at the end of the tour — free samples of beer (soft drinks for children) served in the beer gardens. Wear comfortable shoes for climbing stairs and coats for walking between buildings. Children under 18 are welcome with parents or guardians; no strollers are permitted.

Miller Brewery
4251 West State Street (931-2153)

- Walk-in tours Monday-Friday, hourly 9am-3pm and at 3:30pm; April-October open Saturday; closed Sunday and major holidays.
- Groups of 15 or more people must make reservations 48 hours in advance (931-2151).
- Parking one block west of Tour Center.
- Handicapped visitors see a 12-minute multi-media presentation and are escorted to the Miller Inn to wait for the rest of their group.

A polka band adds "oomph" to the beer garden on Wednesdays and Saturdays in the summer at the Miller Inn.

Pabst Brewery
901 West Juneau Avenue (347-7328).

- Walk-in tours October-April Monday-Friday 10am, 11am, 1pm, 2pm, 3pm, and 3:30 pm; May-September Monday-Saturday hourly tours 9am-3:30pm; closed Sunday and major holidays.
- Parking on the northeast corner of Ninth and Juneau streets.
- Handicapped accessibility in the beer garden only.

You'll be dazzled by the six huge copper kettles dating from 1890-1893.

Cedar Creek Settlement
See "Stone Mill Winery" in Chapter 1.

County Courthouse and Safety Building— Milwaukee County
901 North Ninth Street (278-4971).
- Tours are given Monday-Friday 9am and 1:30pm; closed holidays. Group size 10-25. Call 2-3 weeks in advance to arrange your tour.
- Parking is available in the commercial lot at the north entrance to the courthouse.
- Handicapped accessibility.

There is lots to see! Depending on your timing and luck, you could see a trial or the County Board in session. You may visit the morgue, jail and finger-printing department as well as the District Attorney's office. This tour is recommended for fourth graders and older. The most memorable part of the tour for our kids was going into a jail cell. The tour lasts approximately two hours.

Delco Electronics
7929 South Howell Avenue, Oak Creek 53154 (768-2502).
I-94 to Rawson Avenue exit; east on Rawson Avenue, then south on Howell Avenue.
- Tours given Monday-Friday 9am and 1pm; maximum of 50 people, 12 years of age and older; write 2 weeks in advance to arrange your tour.
- Handicapped accessibility.

It's not what you might expect if someone suggested a trip to a factory. This once-classified electronics plant produces guidance systems for airplanes, missiles, and spacecraft and has only recently been opened for tours. Employees wear uniforms with hoods and gloves to work with the delicate equipment. The clean, quiet environment impressed us.

Fire Stations
Preschoolers are intrigued by firefighters and fire engines. We've noticed older children and adults are too. Most fire stations are happy to show visitors around. Suburban stations are listed by village in the white pages of the telephone directory.

City of Milwaukee Fire Stations
711 West Wells Street (276-5656 ext. 268).
- Tours are given Monday-Friday; maximum group size 25; call at least 48 hours in advance.

Tours of all City of Milwaukee Fire Stations must be arranged through the office of the Fire Chief. Special programs are usually offered during Fire Prevention Week in October.

General Mitchell Field

5300 South Howell Avenue (747-4677).
I-94 to the Airport exit.

- A self-guided walking tour is available; call the Public Relations office in advance and arrange to pick up a copy of the tour.
- Handicapped accessibility.

We've got a big-city airport now and it's impressive! In addition to the excitement of airplanes taking off and landing, this walking tour provides an opportunity to see varied maintenance equipment and the inner workings of an airport. If your group is coming by bus, ask about a visit to the Airport Firehouse. This is the highlight of most children's tours. Call ahead to any airline to coordinate an additional tour through an airplane. Park in "Long Term Parking"; it's $1.50 per day. ("Short Term Parking" can cost up to $5.00.)

Green Meadows Farm

P.O. Box 182, Waterford 53185 (414/534-2891).
I-94 exit west Racine-Waterford; travel 18 miles on Highway 20. The farm is located 30 minutes southeast of Milwaukee.

- Tours daily 10am-4pm, April 1-November 15.
- Admission, fee.
- Two restaurants and picnic grounds are on the premises.
- Handicapped accessibility; the staff is very accommodating, willing to put wheelchairs in the haywagons and give special help to pony riders.

A great way for a city kid — young or old — to see a farm. Fulfill your farm fantasies: jump in a haystack, feed the goats (baby bottles supplied), see the cows at milking time, and ride a pony. Friendly farm animals abound for you to pet. These people are pros at running a farm tour. For a great October outing, plan to pick a pumpkin and prepare it for Halloween.

▶ Special feature: For a moo-ving experience, remember that June is Dairy Month, a perfect time to tour a working dairy farm. The Waukesha County June Dairy Month Committee sponsors these tours which usually include milking demonstrations and free dairy products. Look for announcements in area newspapers.

Honey Acres

Highway 67, Ashippun (414/474-4411).
Exit I-43 north at Highway 67; north of New Ashippun.

- Open 9am-3pm weekdays year-round; open weekends in summer.
- Group tours offered; call 2 weeks in advance.
- Handicapped accessibility.

See the bees, a 20-minute slideshow, the nature trail, and the bee-keeping museum. The honey is great! Your outing might be combined with a trip to Holy Hill (see Chapter 1) or to North Lake (see Chapter 6) to see the Kettle Moraine Scenic Steam Train.

Hospitals

Hospitals are a natural trip for a school group. You might also think about it for a Scout trip, birthday party, or church activity.

Children's Hospital
1700 West Wisconsin Avenue (931-4043).
- Group tours Tuesday and Thursday 9:45am and 1:30pm; arrange tours 2 weeks in advance; maximum tour size 35 children.
- Handicapped accessibility.

Children assume doctor and patient roles as they try on surgical masks and gowns, sit in a hospital bed, look at X-rays, and examine some of the medical apparatus. This "Hospital Orientation for Children" is suited to ages preschool to 8. Allow one hour for the tour.

St Luke's Hospital
2900 West Oklahoma Avenue (649-6521).
- Group tours of the Pediatric Department are given by appointment only for grades K-2; maximum tour size 30 children and requires 4 adults.
- Drop-in "Pre-Operation Tour" for children Wednesdays at 7pm.
- Handicapped accessibility.

This is a popular tour; call six to twelve months in advance to ensure your specific date. The two-day program begins with a visit by the hospital staff to your group and includes role-playing. The second day is an on-site tour featuring a memorable performance by Mr. Yuk.

St. Michael Hospital
2400 West Villard Avenue (527-8275).
West on Villard Avenue off Green Bay Avenue.
- Children's orientations are given only during the school year on Wednesdays at 9am for ages 5-9; maximum group of 25 with at least 2 adults; call 4 weeks in advance.
- Family-centered maternity tours one Sunday afternoon each month; call for date and time.
- Handicapped accessibility.

This hospital orientation for children includes a Mr. Rogers film and the opportunity to dress up in gowns, shoes, masks, and all the accouterments. Children leave with a souvenir grab bag of tongue depressors, adhesive bandages, etc. Allow two hours.

Humane Society Animal Shelter

4151 North Humboldt Boulevard (961-0310).
Two blocks north of Capitol Drive.
- Tours Monday-Friday 10am-4pm; call in advance.
- Handicapped accessibility.

Designed for animal lovers, this one-hour tour of the shelter is planned for kindergarten age and older. Delight in lots of winsome kittens, puppies (some for adoption), and the resident rabbits.

Marshall and Ilsley Bank

770 North Water street (765-7537).

- Tours Monday-Friday 9am-2pm; call 2 weeks in advance. Tours are not available the 1st, 2nd, 3rd, 15th, 16th or 30th of the month.
- Parking is available in the Customer Parking Center on Wells Street, one block east of Water Street.
- Handicapped accessibility with advanced notice.

School-age children can see how a bank operates when they tour this oldest Wisconsin bank (1839). They will see the safety deposit vault, the mail room, and other selected operations. The extensive collection of Owen Gromme's wildlife paintings will delight any age. A seasonal treat is the Christmas display of life-sized Steiff stuffed animals in the lobby.

The Milwaukee Journal/Sentinel

333 West State Street (224-2120).

- Tours Monday-Friday 10am and 2pm by reservation only; group size 15-30 people, ages 12 and older; call 2 weeks in advance.
- Parking in commercial lots.

The roar of the presses impresses! Time your visit to get the full effect. There's lots of walking and miles of newsprint. The display on the fifth floor showing how to print a color picture is worth a close look. Allow 70 minutes for the tour.

Milwaukee Railroad Station (Amtrak)

433 West St. Paul Street (271-0840).

- Group tours are available Monday-Friday 9am-5pm; call in advance.
- Handicapped accessibility.

This 20-30 minute tour is tailored to the age of your group. Each tour includes the baggage and ticket areas. It may be possible to climb aboard a train, although rides are not provided.

See the Chicago section in Chapter 6 for our suggestions for traveling to Chicago by train. It's a good way to go!

Orlandini Studio Ltd.

633 West Virginia Street (272-3657).
At the south side of the Sixth Street viaduct.

- Tours given by appointment only and may be arranged at a mutually convenient time; adults only; maximum group size is 15.

If there is decorative plasterwork in your home, you may well recognize the molds in this shop. Orlandini is a second-generation artist and another fine Milwaukee craftsman. His studio is a working shop; everything is covered with a fine layer of white plaster dust (don't wear navy blue). The molds, process, and delicacy of the designs fascinated us. Orlandini's love of his craft shows in the pieces he creates and is communicated during the tour.

Paramedics

When "Stop-Drop-And-Roll" is taught by a paramedic, your children are likely to remember this life-saving procedure. Paramedics encourage these tours so you can become acquainted with them and see what they do and how they do it. If you ever need their help, it's nice to have already met.

North Shore Paramedics
5900 North Milwaukee River Parkway; located in the Glendale Fire Department (228-1565).
- Tours given 8am-11am and 1pm-4pm; call the shift captain 48 hours in advance to arrange your tour; maximum group 30 people.
- Handicapped accessibility.

Milwaukee Paramedics
- Tours by appointment only (276-5656).

Wauwatosa Paramedics
10525 Watertown Plank Road (453-8600).
- Tours by appointment only.

West Allis Paramedics
7310 West National Avenue (476-7531).
- Tours by appointment only; no tours on Mondays. Call the captain at Station No. 1.

Police

Milwaukee Police Department and Milwaukee Police Academy Tours are offered weekdays, by written request only. Write 2 weeks in advance to Personnel Bureau, Milwaukee Police Department, P.O. Box 531, Milwaukee, Wisconsin 53201.

Milwaukee Police Department
749 West State Street (273-8660 ext. 448).
- Handicapped accessibility.

Milwaukee Police Academy
6680 North Teutonia Avenue (273-8660 ext. 448).

Visitors to the State Street station will see the detective bureau, photo laboratory, fingerprinting equipment, and the computer center. Children like the motorcycle/equipment room, and the jail always intrigues. The Police Academy tour includes the rifle range, a firearms display, and three-dimensional crime scenes.

We recommend that younger children visit a local police station where police officers will talk to them about what they do. For listings of Milwaukee district police stations, see "Milwaukee — City of: Police" in the white pages of the telephone directory.

Television Stations

How do they put the picture in the box? A tour of a television studio will explain the process and include a view of the studio and technical equipment. Some stations will accommodate groups with special interests.

WTMJ-TV 4
720 East Capitol Drive (332-9611 ext. 320).
- Group tours Monday-Friday 10:30am and 1:30pm; maximum group size of 30, ages 8 and older.
- Handicapped accessibility.

WITI-TV 6
9001 North Green Bay Road (355-6666).
- Group tours Monday-Friday 9:30am-5:30pm; group size 15-30 people ages 9 and older; call 2-3 months in advance.
- Handicapped accessibility.

WMVS-TV 10 / WMVT-TV 36
1036 North Eighth Street (271-1036).
At Eighth Street and Highland Boulevard, part of the M.A.T.C. campus.
- Group tours Monday-Friday 9am-4pm for 15-30 people, ages 8 and up; call 2 weeks in advance.
- Special arrangements may be made for a family group.
- Handicapped accessibility.

WISN-TV 12
759 North Nineteenth Street (342-8812).
Two blocks north of Wisconsin Avenue.
- Group tours Wednesday-Thursday 9-11:30am and 12:30-2pm; group size 5-15 people, ages 10 and older; call 7 days in advance.

WVTV-TV 18
4041 North Thirty-Fifth Street (442-7050).
One half-block north of Capitol Drive.
- Group tours Monday, Tuesday, Wednesday and Friday 1-4:30pm; group size 10-20 people; call 2 weeks in advance.

United States Postal Service

Try a visit to your branch station. Young children enjoy seeing where their mail is sorted for delivery. Contact your local branch through the listings in the white pages of the telephone directory under "United States Government — Postal Service."

Milwaukee Post Office — Main Office
345 West St. Paul Street (291-2350).

- Tours weekdays 9:30am-1pm, Saturdays by special arrangement; call in advance; group size 6 to 50 people; 1 adult required per 10 children under age 16.
- Parking on the street or in the commercial lot across the street; cars illegally parked in the 15-minute lot will be ticketed.
- Handicapped accessibility.

Wisconsin Electric Power Company

Main Plant
231 West Michigan Street (277-2875).

Oak Creek Power Plant
4801 East Elm Road, Oak Creek.

Valley Power Plant
1039 West Canal Street, Milwaukee.

- Group tours only at all 3 plants; call 4 weeks in advance; suitable for ages 12 and up.

Wear flat shoes to climb the stairs; hard hats and safety shields are provided. Tours are offered at all three facilities, but the Oak Creek facility is the largest power plant in Wisconsin and has the most to see. The two-hour tour includes a slide show and visits to the control center, turbine room, and boiler room.

Wisconsin Gas Company

626 East Wisconsin Avenue, 53202 (291-6939).

- Group tours Tuesday-Friday 9am-3pm; ages 13 and older; write 2 weeks in advance to Ms. Nora Collins.
- Parking in commercial lots in the area.
- Handicapped accessibility.

This two-hour tour can be adapted for science projects, career talks, or general information. To eat lunch in the cafeteria, ask about the special arrangements when you write to request the tour.

3
Back To Nature

Boerner Botanical Gardens (Whitnall Park)

5879 South 92nd Street, Hales Corners 53130 (425-1130).
Enter on 92nd Street, ½ mile south of Grange Avenue.

- Open daily 8am-sunset. April 15-October.
- Admission, fee.
- Guided tours Monday-Friday, adults only, fee; write for reservation 3 weeks in advance.
- Gift shop.

These spectacular formal and informal gardens are a blaze of color mid-June through September. But you can also enjoy a springtime visit to the Rock Garden where Wisconsin wild flowers are in bloom; look for the trillium, hepatica, and jack-in-the-pulpit. The formal rose gardens reach peak color in mid-June. Wander from the formal rose gardens over the Bog Bridge to the nature trail; allow one hour. For a small fee, you may purchase a trail guide.

In the summer, a weekly evening concert is held in the formal gardens; this is a popular event and admission is free. Bring a picnic supper to eat in nearby Whitnall Park, then enjoy the concert. There are a variety of art displays and lectures throughout the year. Need a plant doctor? The horticulturist is available in the summer to answer your questions; call for an appointment.

Send a self-addressed stamped envelope for a calendar of events.

Feed the Ducks

Lincoln Memorial Drive, just north of the Milwaukee Art Museum.

You can do it year-round; the lagoon is aerated to prevent freezing! Kids love it here in fall and winter when great numbers of ducks are in residence. The squawking and quacking is deafening. Bring your old bread and they'll gobble it down. In spring and summer, watch for newly hatched ducklings.

Green Meadows Farm

See "Behind the Scenes" in Chapter 2.

Honey Acres

See "Behind the Scenes" in Chapter 2.

Milwaukee County Department of Parks, Recreation and Culture

901 North Ninth Street, County Courthouse Room 301 (278-4345).

The parks offer more than just picnicking and strolling. Did you know that the 137 parks offer 16 golf courses, 39 wading pools, 17 outdoor pools, 3 indoor pools, over 76 miles of bike trails, 3 exercise courses, numerous hiking trails, 134 tennis courts (53 lighted), and 3 downhill ski areas? And if that doesn't impress you, try the Boerner Botanical Gardens in Whitnall Park. The formal gardens, the bog and the wildflowers make it one of our favorite places. The county park system also includes the Lakefront, which provides spectacular vistas and is the city's favorite playground.

The facilities available vary from park to park. Call for rate information and calendar of monthly events (278-4345). The "Parks 'n' Places" discount club (963-1233) offers reduced rates for park activities.

Special features:

▶ **Picnic permits** are issued at the Public Service Office in Room 301 in the Milwaukee County Courthouse (278-4333). A minimum of three days notice is required, though large groups must reserve months in advance. Small groups with beer privilege for 10 or fewer people must reserve at the individual park only; fee.

▶ **Senior citizen programs.** "Seniors Only" centers are located at Washington Park, Wilson Park, and Rose Park; multi-purpose centers are at King Park and Kosciuszko Park. Noon meals are served at nutrition sites on weekdays at Wilson and Rose parks. Membership in recreation programs, age 55 and older, costs only $2.00. Call for program information (933-2332).

▶ **Handicapped citizens programs.** Two year-round Wil-O-Way Centers offer recreation services for persons with physical, emotional, and developmental disabilities:

Wil-O-Way Recreation Center (771-1100)
10602 Underwood Parkway, Wauwatosa 53226

Wil-O-Way Grant Recreation Center (762-2324)
207 Lake Drive, South Milwaukee 53172

The Easter Seal Society sponsors summer programs at Holler Park for the physically handicapped of all ages. Transportation is provided. Call 482-0133.

▶ **The Park People** is a citizen support group working to promote public appreciation and support of Milwaukee's county park system. Through "discovery" programs for members and the public, active involvement in park development and preservation, gift opportunities and park advocacy, Park People is contributing to the continued high quality of Milwaukee's parks. Membership in this volunteer nonprofit corporation is open to all (332-PARK).

County parks at a glance

Park	YOUTH CENTER	WADING POOL	TOBOGGAN SLIDES	TENNIS	SWIMMING-OUTDOOR	SWIMMING-INDOOR	SOFTBALL	SOCCER	SENIOR CENTER	ROOM RENTAL	PLAY EQUIPMENT	PICNIC AREA	NATURE TRAIL	ICE SKATING	HANDICAPPED CENTER	GOLF COURSE	FORMAL GARDENS	FOOTBALL	FOOD CONCESSION	FISHING	EXERCISE COURSE	DOWN HILL SKIING	CROSS COUNTRY SKI TRAIL	COMMUNITY CENTER	BOAT LAUNCHING	BIKE TRAIL	BEACH	BASKETBALL	BASEBALL	BANDSHELL	ARCHERY
BAY VIEW																										•	•				
BROWN DEER				•			•	•			•	•	•	•		•					•	•		•			•			•	
CANNON	•	•			•	•		•	•			•																•			
CARVER		•						•																				•			
CHEROKEE				•				•	•		•	•		•					•									•	•		
COOPER		•					•	•	•	•																		•			
CURRIE																•					•	•	•								
DINEEN		•		•	•		•	•			•	•			•													•	•		
DOCTORS								•			•	•	•	•													•				
DOYNE							•												•									•			
DRETZKA			•													•					•		•								
ESTABROOK				•			•	•			•	•	•					•			•				•						
FALK											•	•		•																	
GORDON	•			•							•	•															•				
GRANT		•			•		•	•			•	•		•				•	•					•	•				•		
GREENFIELD								•			•													•			•		•		
HALES CORNERS		•		•	•		•	•			•	•	•							•								•	•		
HOLLER								•																					•		
HOYT				•																		•									
HUMBOLDT		•						•	•	•		•								•								•	•		
JACKSON							•	•	•		•	•	•																•		
JACOBUS								•			•	•																	•		
KING	•							•			•	•																			
KINNICKINNIC RIVER PKWY.			•								•	•															•	•	•		•
KLETZSCH												•													•						•
KOSCIUSZKO	•	•						•	•		•	•	•											•		•			•		
LaFOLLETTE								•																					•		
LAKE				•			•	•			•	•	•			•		•		•							•			•	
LINCOLN				•	•		•	•			•	•	•					•		•								•	•		
LINCOLN CREEK PKWY.							•											•										•	•		•
MADISON																												•	•		
McCARTY		•			•		•	•			•	•		•						•								•	•		
McGOVERN	•						•	•			•	•		•														•	•		
McKINLEY																				•				•	•	•					
MITCHELL					•			•			•					•	•												•		
MOODY		•						•			•																		•		
NOYES			•		•	•		•																				•	•		
OAK CREEK PKWY.								•			•	•	•					•									•		•		
OAKWOOD																•			•												
PULASKI-MILWAUKEE		•		•			•	•			•	•																•	•		
RAINBOW																												•			
ROOT RIVER PKWY.							•																			•		•	•		•
ROSE																											•				
SCOUT LAKE								•			•	•			•						•								•		
SHERIDAN		•	•		•																•							•			
SHERMAN	•	•						•			•																		•		
SMITH								•			•							•											•		
SOUTH SHORE				•				•			•														•		•	•			
TIEFENTHALER		•						•			•	•		•												•			•		
UNDERWOOD CREEK PKWY.																															•
WARNIMONT	•			•							•		•					•										•			
WASHINGTON	•	•		•	•			•			•	•									•					•		•	•	•	
WHITNALL		•	•		•		•	•			•	•	•			•		•					•	•			•				
WILSON																				•									•		

Mitchell Park Horticultural Conservatory (The Domes)

524 South Layton Boulevard, 53215 (649-9800).
I-94 West, exit south on 27th Street, which becomes Layton Boulevard.

- September-May, open Monday-Friday 9am-5pm, Saturday-Sunday 9am-8pm; June-August, Saturday-Thursday 9am-8pm, Friday 9am-5pm.
- Admission, fee; Milwaukee County residents with I.D., free 9am-10:30am, Monday-Friday (not including major holidays); handicapped free with I.D.
- Free parking.
- Group tours available for 20 or more; send a self-addressed stamped envelope for information.
- No food service; the park is delightful, bring a picnic.
- Gift shop.
- Handicapped accessibility.

Everyone in Milwaukee recognizes these geodesic domes. Each is almost the height of a seven-story building and half the length of a football field. Inside, you'll find two-and-a-half acres of growing space under glass. The Show Dome is a "show stopper" with its seasonal displays. The colors are spectacular on any day, but are especially soul-soothing on a gray winter day. While wandering in the Arid Dome, note the Saguaro cactus; it's 150 years old. In the Tropical Dome, look up! Orchids grow everywhere, even among the branches of the 65-foot tall Kapok tree. The favorite spot for the kids is the waterfall; bring lots of pennies to make wishes. Children in strollers are welcome.

Special features:
▶ Send a self-addressed stamped envelope for a calendar of events, including the dates for the spring, summer, fall, Christmas, and winter shows.
▶ Having a party? The Domes can be rented. Call for information.
▶ Look for the Greenhouse Plant Sale in May and November. For that lonely spot in your house, try the Exotic Plant Sale in October.

Nature Preserves and Community Parks

We suspect there are numerous local nature preserves and parks within Milwaukee County that we haven't found. From the quality of the three nature preserves we've discovered, we recommend you be on the lookout for more.

Cudahy Nature Preserve
On College Avenue east of Howell Avenue (761-1151, tours 425-8551).

Hawthorne Glen Nature Preserve
1130 North 60th Street (475-5300).

Shorewood Nature Preserve
3600 North Lake Drive (332-4200).

Riveredge Nature Center

4438 West Hawthorne Drive, Newburg (414/931-8095).
Just east of Newburg, on the Milwaukee River; Highway 33 to County Highway Y.

- Open weekdays 3pm-dusk, weekends 8am-sunset.
- Admission for nonmembers, fee payable in the parking lot.
- Group tours available, call for information.

The hiking trail meanders along the banks of the Milwaukee River, offering some lovely views. Hang onto the kids; the cliffs are high in some places. Bridges crisscross lowland sections of swamp. Bird-watching here is great. The sugar maples are tapped in the spring. It's a treat for kids to see the huge black kettles on tripods with the maple syrup boiling over the open fire. Wonderful smells!

The nature center encourages your membership in order to participate in all the family-oriented programs, such as the Harvest Festival, the Pancake Breakfasts, and snowshoeing. The hiking trails are open to the public.

Schlitz Audubon Center

1111 East Brown Deer Road (352-2880).

- Open Tuesday-Sunday 9am-5pm; closed Thanksgiving weekend, Christmas Day, and New Year's Day.
- Nonmember admission, fee; members, free.
- Guided and self-guided tours available.
- No food service, no picnicking.
- Natural history bookstore with gifts for nature lovers.

These 187 beautiful acres on Lake Michigan have beach, meadows, ponds, and woods. And to think this place is only a few minutes from the city! Once the domain of the Joseph Schlitz Brewing Company's horses, this lovely acreage remains undeveloped and today offers a tranquil respite from the city. See for yourself in the spring when the trillium bloom. In winter, cross-country skiing here makes a great outing.

There are unadvertised drop-in programs on weekends from May through August. Enjoy a talk with the naturalist. Members of the Schlitz Audubon Center (minimum $15.00 per family) and the National Audubon Society receive free admission and the newsletter/calendar, which lists the excellent programs available.

Shoots and Roots

929 North Sixth Street (224-4866).

Don't overlook the easiest escape — your own backyard! To help you plan that vegetable garden you've always dreamed about, here's a fantastic program. This co-operative effort of the Milwaukee County Extension Service and the University of Wisconsin-Extension will teach you how to grow, serve and preserve your own fruits and vegetables. Call to register for the free informative newsletters which have featured everything from a "Squash Vine Borer Alert" to a recipe for Swiss Chard Pie.

Todd Wehr Nature Center (in Whitnall Park)

5879 South 92nd Street, Hales Corners 53130 (425-8550).
Enter on College Avenue between 92nd Street and Highway 100.

- Open November 1-April 30 Monday-Saturday 8am-4:30pm; May 1-October 31 daily 8am-4:30pm.
- School tours available; call for information.
- Gift shop — something special for nature buffs.

Here's a spot we return to again and again. It's a "living laboratory" with 200 acres of prairies, wetlands, oak savannahs, and a lake. Enjoy the wild flowers and watch for a variety of birds. Take a Sunday morning hike with one of the naturalists. There are printed guides which are helpful and may be purchased for a small fee at the Nature Center where the four miles of tours begin and end. The maps are free.

This family-oriented preserve has seasonal programs throughout the year with workshops and clubs for every interest. One of our favorites is "Bug Day" where the whole family learns how to catch and collect insects. Watch for the Camera Club's exhibits of members' outstanding nature photos — truly professional quality. There's usually a crowd of kids around the glass-enclosed beehive. The innovative beekeeper has made it easy to spot the queen. Look for the tiny "white out" dot.

Special features:
▶ A newsletter is published seasonally listing all programs; cost, $2.00. A bargain for park lovers!
▶ Watch the newspapers for weekend family programs, which require preregistration and payment of a small fee.
▶ Four miles of cross-country ski trails are open for wintertime visits; no trail fees.

Wisconsin State Parks/Wisconsin Department of Natural Resources

2300 North Third Street, P.O. Box 12436, Milwaukee 53212.
(562-9500 campsite information, 799-1300 recorded message).

We are indebted to the continental glaciers which carved a magnificent geological variety of glorious landscapes across much of Wisconsin. Our state parks offer rugged shorelines, sandy beaches, Indian burial grounds, rivers, gorges, waterfalls, woodlands bluffs and prairies. Take your pick.

The best brochure we have found is free, and is updated every year. Every state park, address, telephone number and a complete list of facilities is on one page. Call 562-9500 and ask for the Visitor's Guide, publication #4-8400(84). For a first-hand look at what there is to see and do year-round in Wisconsin's state parks, photojournalist and outdoorsman Jim Umhoeffer's *All Season Guide to Wisconsin's Parks, Forests, Recreation Areas and Trails* offers informative commentaries, expressive photographs and easy-to-use maps. (Northword, P.O. Box 5634, Madison, WI 53705)

Camping

Campsite applications are available at four locations in the Milwaukee area. Send a self-addressed stamped envelope or pick up an application in person. (Or write to Department of Natural Resources, Box 7921, Madison, WI 53707.)

- Milwaukee Public Library, 814 West Wisconsin Avenue, Milwaukee 53233.
- Waukesha Public Library, 321 Wisconsin Avenue, Waukesha 53186.
- Wisconsin Department of Natural Resources, 2300 North Third Street, P.O. Box 12436, Milwaukee 53212.
- Ozaukee Public Library, 11345 North Cedarburg Road, Highway 60 West, Mequon 53092.

Campsite applications for reserved sites are accepted by mail only as of January 1. The daily fees are reasonable. The middle of winter is the best time to plan your summer. If you wait for warm weather to make your plans, you may have trouble obtaining a site. Unreserved sites are limited and often unavailable during the camping season.

See Chapter 8, Escape from Milwaukee, for the locations of state parks within a 150-mile radius of Milwaukee: Aztalan, Governor Dodge, Kettle Moraine, and Kohler-Andrae.

Zoo—Milwaukee County

10001 West Bluemound Road (771-3040).
Intersection of I-94 and Highway 45.

- Open May 5-Labor Day daily 9am-5pm, Sunday and holidays 9am-6pm; after Labor Day daily 9am-4:30pm; closed Christmas and New Year's Day.
- Admission, fee; Milwaukee County residents with identification Monday-Friday 9am-11am, free; handicapped, free.
- Guided and self-guided tours are available, as is a motorized tour; call in advance.
- Groups of 20 or more people, call for special rates.
- Parking lot, fee; parking on the street is hard to find.
- Restaurant and snack bar; picnicking allowed.
- Gift shop.
- Handicapped accessibility; buildings and walkways are easily managed. Strollers for children and adults may be rented.

The beautifully designed walkways allow you to see the entire zoo comfortably in one visit. Moated areas provide an unobstructed view of the animals in a predator/prey relationship. Birds soar overhead in the Aviary, and gorillas enjoy the Great Ape Escape, their recently opened outdoor playground. Chandar, a white Bengal tiger, moves with elegance and grace in a setting imitative of his natural surroundings.

A not-to-be-missed attraction for all ages is the Children's Zoo, which is open from Memorial Day weekend to Labor Day. This charming area allows for close interaction between children and animals. Watching the children feed the goats, you might wonder who is having the most fun. Each day finds new animal guests of honor. Here's your chance to make nose-to-nose contact with the animals and chat with their attendants. You may meet a baby elephant or a kinkajou, pet a snake or cuddle a new animal friend.

Consider a train ride when you arrive at the zoo. You'll get a nice overview of the grounds, though there may be a wait for this popular attraction. Check the schedule for departure times. You'll find the open-air train to the left of the Zoo entrance.

The Zoo is a treat in any season and abounds in activity year-round. Cross-country ski trails wind through the park; ski equipment can be rented and instruction is available. See "Skiing" in chapters 3 and 4.

On a Sunday in mid-January, participate in "Samson's Stomp," a six-mile run. "My Heart's at the Zoo" is in February — bring a valentine for your favorite animal. Mid-June is "Teddy Bear Days." Enjoy bear tours and the three-meter "Baby Bear Crawl." Small bands play on summer weekends in the daytime. Background music for the animal sounds is also provided by the evening Miller Summer Series of concerts, which includes appearances by the Milwaukee Symphony Orchestra. Sit in the tent or bring a blanket. We found it a delightful excuse for an elaborate picnic supper

4
The Sporting Life

Spectator Sports

Baseball
• Milwaukee County Stadium ticket office (933-1818) is open weekdays 9am-5pm.
• Tickets may be purchased through Ticketron with Mastercard or Visa (933-9000).

County Stadium is home to the Brewers from April through September. Day games begin at 1:30pm weekdays; nighttime games start at 7:30pm. Be sure to check your tickets for daytime and twilight doubleheader times. And if all these times confuse you, consider starting two hours prior to game time when the parking lot is open for Milwaukee's famous tailgate parties. Call the County Park Service (344-1800); large group parties can reserve areas. Season tickets go on sale in mid-November.

Basketball
Bucks
• Arena ticket office (272-8080).

The Bucks, Milwaukee's professional basketball team, take to the court at the Milwaukee Arena from late October through May. Games start at 7:30pm Monday through Thursday; Friday and Saturday at 8pm; Sunday game times may vary. Lots of the good seats go to season ticket purchasers, so tickets for individual games can be scarce. For best choices, buy your tickets in September or October, even for individual seating.

Marquette Warriors
• Individual tickets may be purchased in the ticket office (224-7127) at 1212 West Wisconsin Avenue. Watch for special notices in the papers at the beginning of October.

Also playing in the Milwaukee Arena are the Marquette University Warriors. Their season runs from mid-November through March. Games are Saturday at 8pm, week nights at 7pm. These exciting collegiate games draw almost as many fans as the pros — there is a waiting list of 1,800 for season tickets.

Bicycle Racing
The skill and stamina of the cyclists from the United States, Canada, and Europe are impressive as they compete in the *Milwaukee Sentinel* Cycling Classic each July. The best place to see it all is at the Lakefront. The crowds shout encouragement as the cyclists streak past, spokes flashing, wheels humming. Sprinklers along the route cool the racers down; a pace car stays ahead of the leaders, and the pack keeps moving. Watch for the sprint at the finish line. Race routes are published in the newspapers in July. Admission, free.

Boxing

It's not just who's in the ring, but who's in the audience. The Golden Gloves Amateur Boxing is held during February and March at the Eagles Club, 2401 West Wisconsin Avenue. During the winter months, the Eagles Club also hosts the Toughman Contests. These "survival of the fittest" competitions are not for the faint at heart. Admission, fee.

Football

- Call the Packer Ticket Office (342-2717) for information concerning games played in Milwaukee.

The Green Bay Packers play some of their home games at Lambeau Field in Green Bay and the balance of them at Milwaukee County Stadium. The regular season is September through December. There are four preseason games in August. Game times vary; check your tickets. Season tickets are a sellout, although a few individual seats may be available by mail-order only.

Hockey

- Tickets may be purchased at the ticket office (225-2400) at 710 North Plankinton Avenue or through Ticketron.

The action is fast-moving and sometimes tempers flare when the Milwaukee Admirals play. Their games are at the Milwaukee Arena; their season is from mid-October until May. Game time is 7:30pm weekdays, 4:30pm Sundays.

Polo

Milwaukee Polo Club

If you haven't been to a match, try it; the whole family will enjoy the fast action on the field. There are two polo leagues in the Milwaukee area. The Milwaukee Polo Club plays its games at Uihlein Field, 7100 West Good Hope Road. Matches are generally held on Sunday afternoons, and an admission fee is charged; children under 12, free. Watch the newspapers for times.

Olympic Polo Club

The Olympic Polo Club meets on the grounds of the Olympia Resort in Oconomowoc. New members are actively being recruited for the men's and women's teams. Spectators are encouraged to bring a picnic lunch and spend the afternoon. You may drive your car up to the edge of the field and spread your blanket. The season runs from late June to August, with matches played on Sunday afternoons; the preliminary match is at 1pm, and the main match is at 3pm.

Rodeo

Rope and romp at the rodeo! Cowboys, broncos, clowns, and bulls return each year in June to the State Fair Park Coliseum. Watch for the date of the Wanago Rodeo. The family favorite is "Kids Hat Day," at the Saturday matinee.

Soccer
UW-M Panthers
- Call (963-4593) for ticket information; ask about group discount rates.

The University of Wisconsin-Milwaukee Panthers play most weekend games at the Bavarian Inn, 700 West Lexington Avenue in Glendale at 2pm. Weekday games are played on campus at Engelman Field, usually at 3:30pm. There is an admission fee charged at the game site.

Wave
- Tickets may be obtained at 749 North Milwaukee Street, Suite 329. Call for information (347-0684).

Did you know Milwaukee has a professional soccer team? The Wave plays its games November-April at the MECCA Auditorium. Home games played Saturday and Sunday afternoons.

Wrestling
- Call the MECCA Auditorium (271-7230) for dates, times and admission prices for the matches.

Participation Sports

Facilities for most every sport are available in the parks or on school playgrounds. Be sure to consult the municipal recreation departments and the "County Parks at a Glance" chart in Chapter 3 for the sporting activity sites in the Milwaukee County park system.

Archery

County sites will provide butts and hay. Be sure to bring your own targets; take your bows and arrows and expect a crowd at all the butts before hunting season.

Baseball

Adults softball leagues abound. The best way to find a league is to ask your friends or coworkers. If that doesn't work, call the County Sports Office (645-8228). For children's teams, call Little League (226-5807).

Biking

Invite a couple friends to hit the "off-the-road" bicycle trails with you. Several bike tour maps have been produced by the G. Heileman Brewing Company and the Milwaukee County Department of Parks, Recreation and Culture. Bike rentals are listed in the Yellow Pages. If you own your bike, be sure to license it in your municipality. If you favor more organized biking activities, call:

- Milwaukee Wheelmen (962-6310).
  2607 North Downer Avenue, Milwaukee 53211.
- Cream City Cycle Club (961-1187).
- Vagabond Ski Club — Summer Activities
  P.O. Box 845, Milwaukee 53201.
- SAABGRAW — *Milwaukee Sentinel* Bike Tours (224-2743).
  P.O. Box 371, Milwaukee 53201 (Fee).

SAABGRAW is more than a bike ride, it's an event! Held each year in August, these three bike tours leave participants glowing. Each tour accommodates only 300 bikers. Applications are accepted after March, and the lottery for positions is held in May. Participants, bikes, and luggage are taken by bus to starting points at Fish Creek, La Crosse, or Wausau for the bike ride back to Milwaukee, covering 60-65 miles each day.

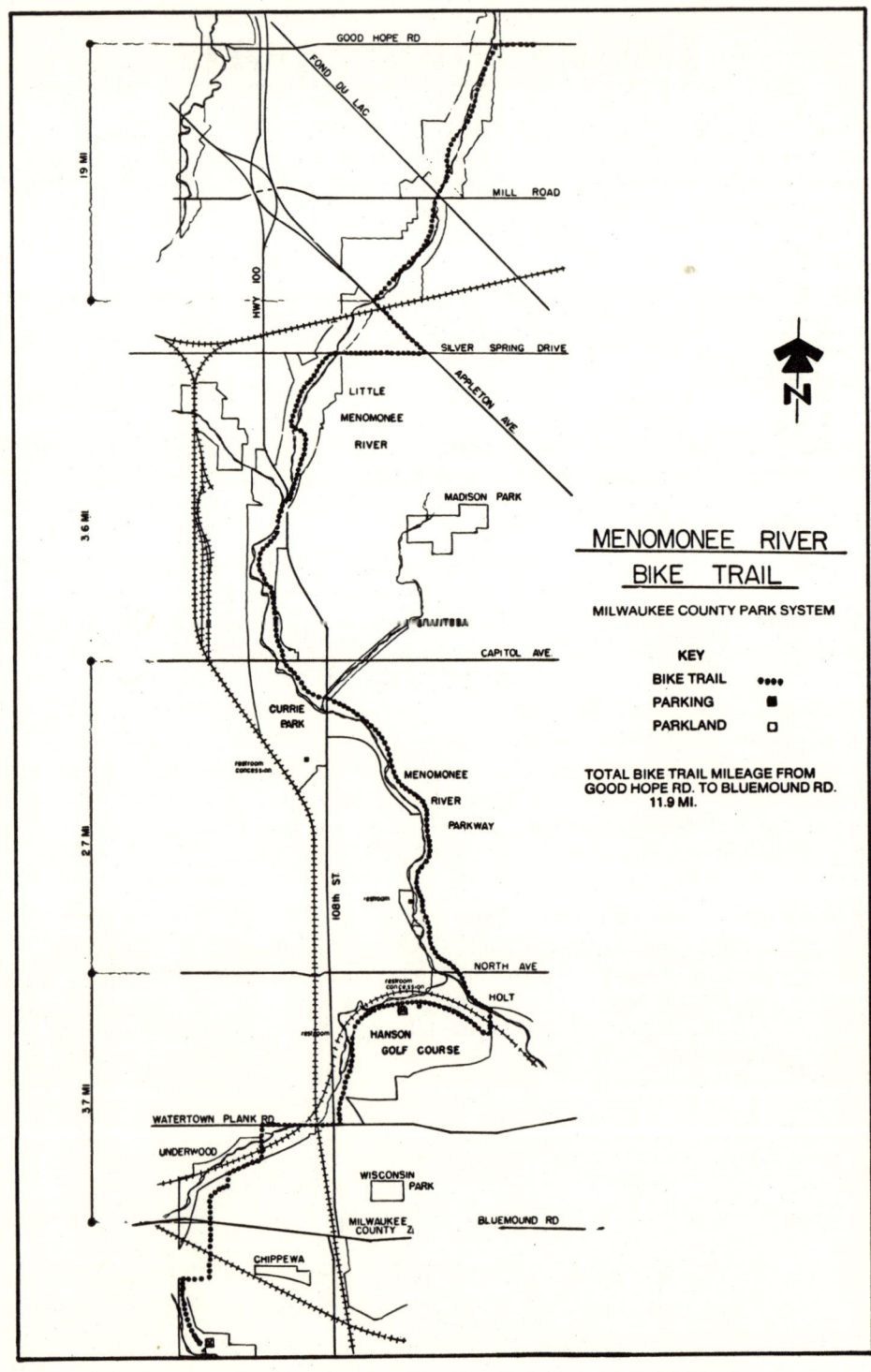

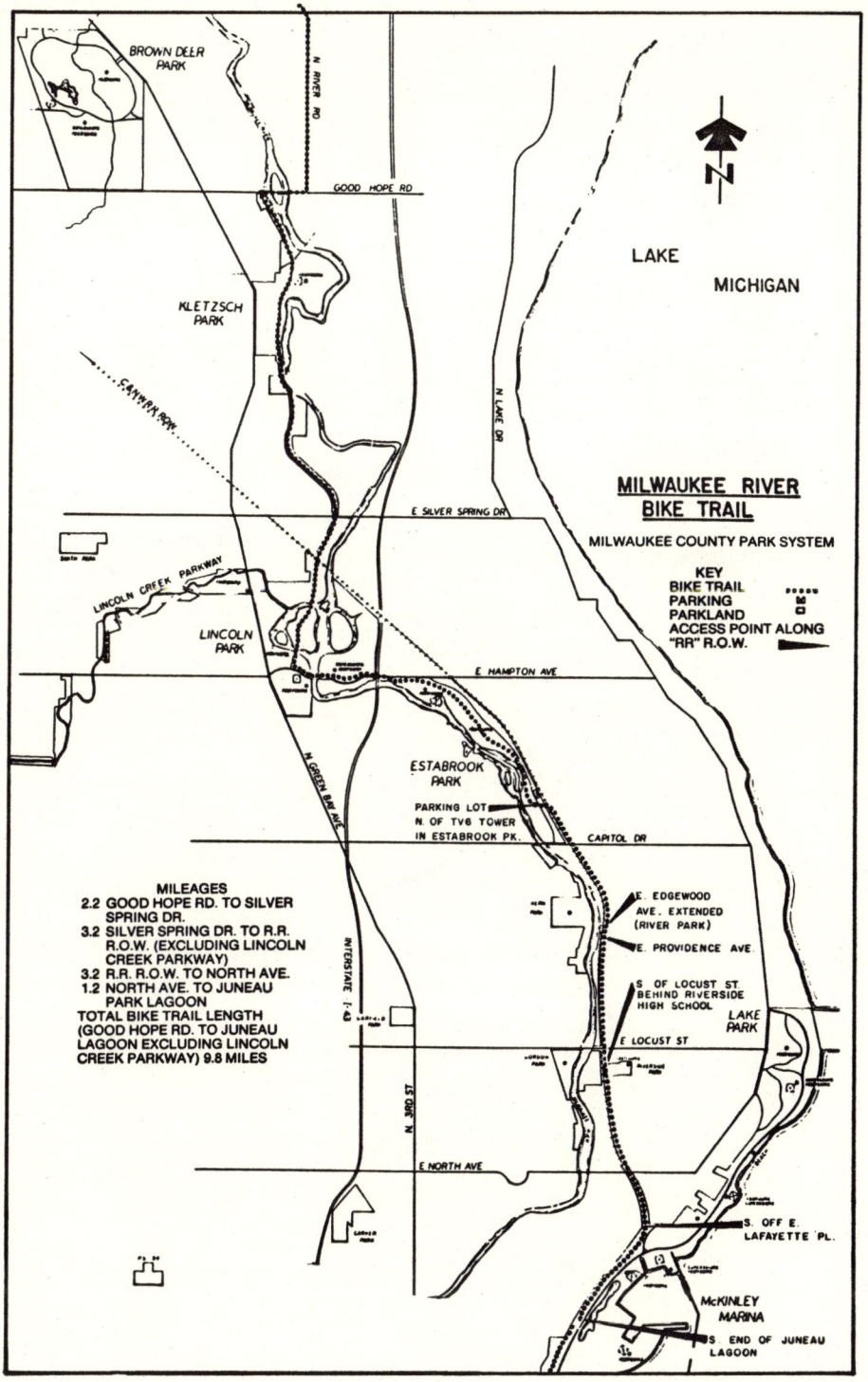

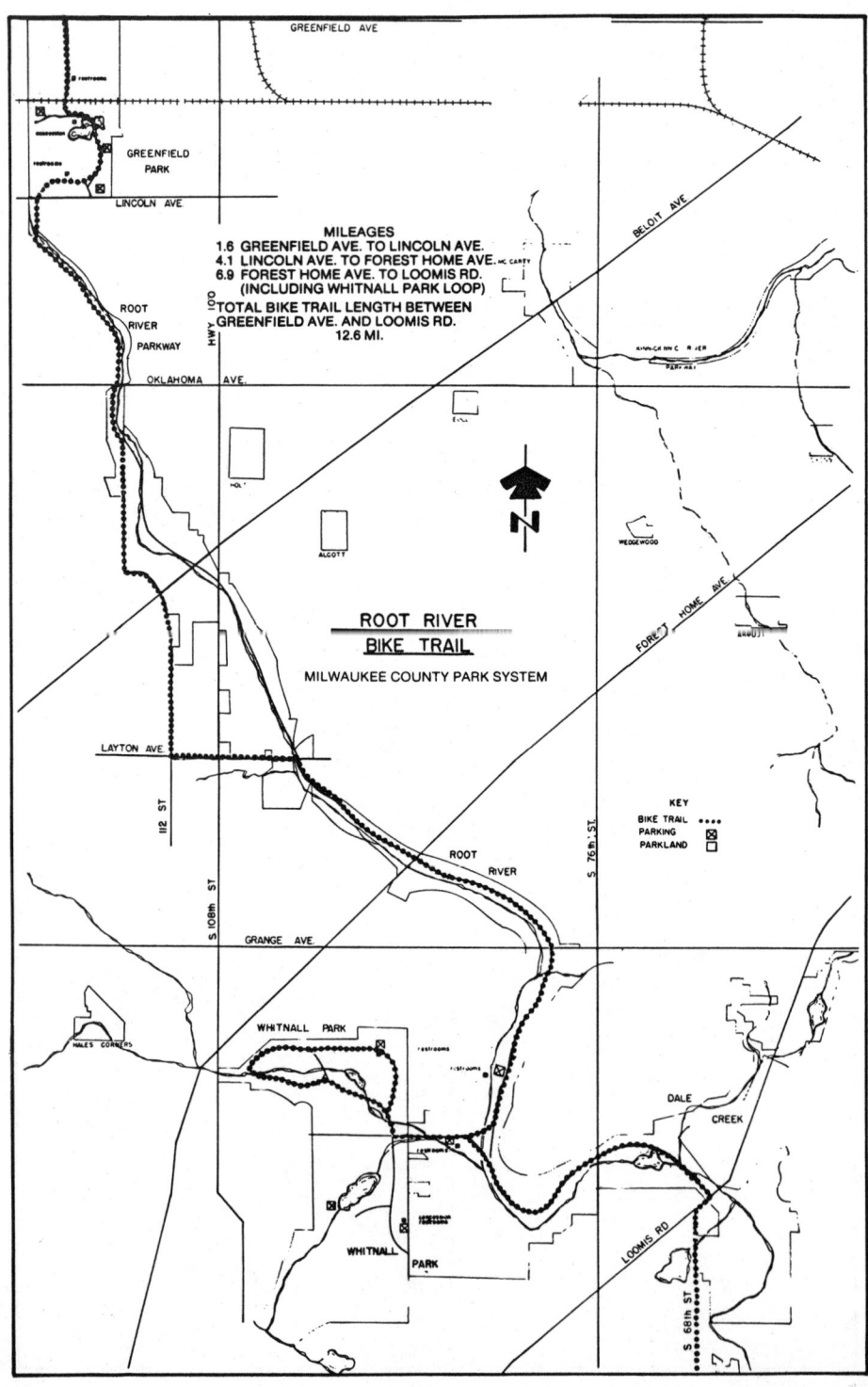

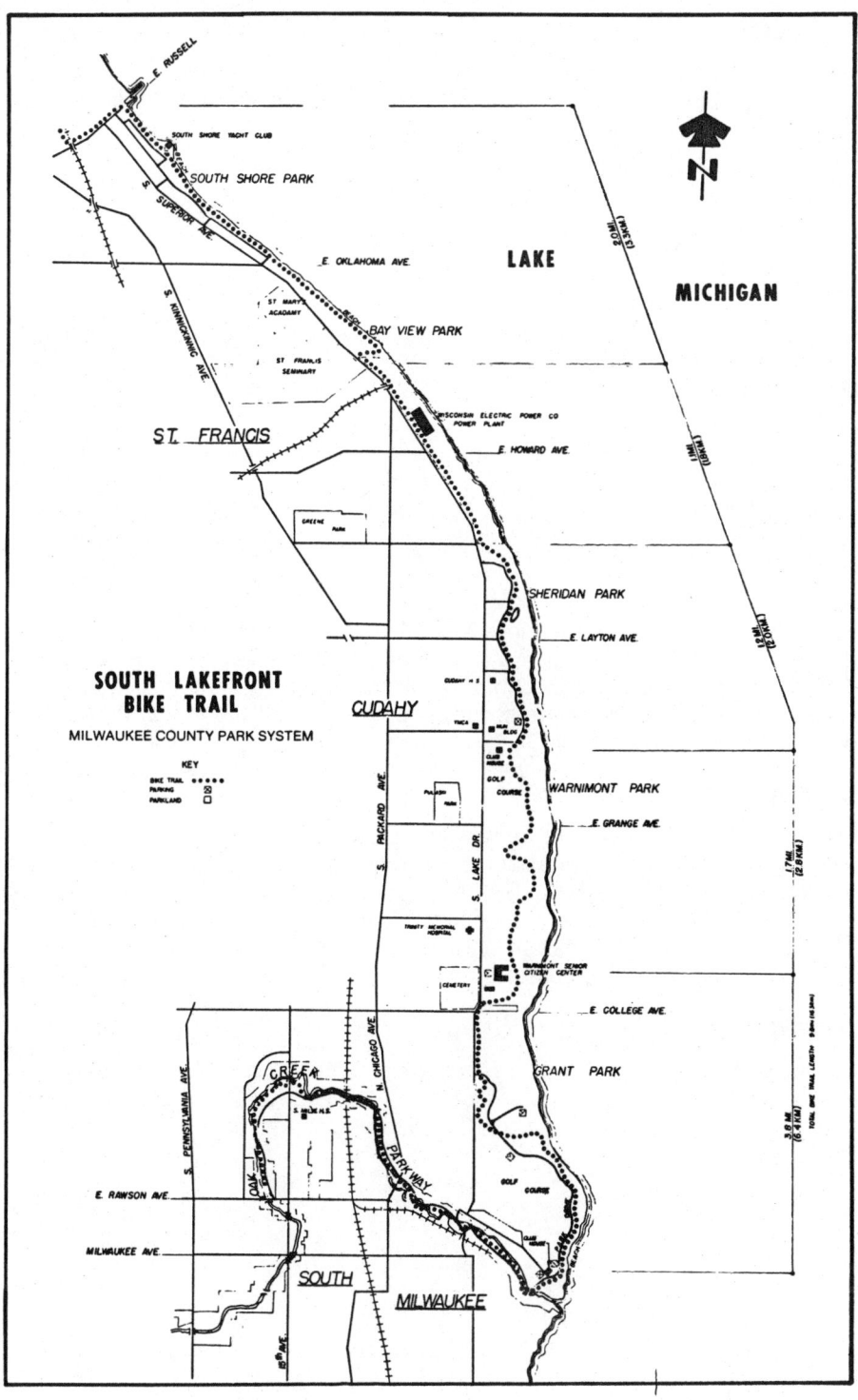

Boating

Opportunities are varied and plentiful. Paddleboats and rowboats may be rented at some park lagoons. For boat launching and slip rental fees, call the Milwaukee County park system (278-4345).
- Milwaukee Rowing Club (964-4772).
- U.S. Coast Guard Auxiliary (781-8558).
  Nonprofit organization promoting boat safety. Free classes, speakers, and films.
- U.S. Power Squadrons
  7336 St. James Street, Wauwatosa 53213.
- Wisconsin Canoe Association (475-7190).
- See also index and below, "Fishing," "Sailing," "Wind Surfing," and "Boat Tours."

Bowling

Indoor
Whether you're rolling gutter balls or making the big strike, you'll want to participate in this popular Milwaukee pastime. Bring the whole family; they'll love it. Consult the Yellow Pages for bowling alleys near you. Call ahead to check league schedules as individual groups are usually not allowed to use the lanes during league time.

Lawn
Here's a little-known sport played in Lake and Dineen parks on Monday, Tuesday, and Thursday evenings and Sundays at 1pm in warm weather. The white-clad players roll elliptical-shaped balls on the manicured greens. It's a friendly sport. The participants love to answer your questions. We found it fun to join the spectators. (There were lots of them.)

Camping

The only camping sites available in Milwaukee County are at State Fair Park. Spaces are limited, but don't be discouraged. If you still want to camp nearby, try the surrounding counties. The Waukesha County Campground includes a sandy beach and several wooded sites. Or try Kettle Moraine or Kohler-Andrae State Parks; there are lots of sites, though only some are wooded, with great hiking and a variety of terrains. See "Wisconsin State Parks" in Chapter 3.

Caving

For information on locations of caves and groups active in caving, write National Speleological Society, Inc. (205/852-1300), Cave Avenue, Huntsville, Alabama 35810. Guided tours are offered at the Cave of the Mounds, Blue Mounds, Wisconsin 53517.

Cross-Country Skiing

See "Skiing, Cross-Country" below.

Curling

Sweep the ice and slide the stone! Get in touch with these area clubs.

- Milwaukee Curling Club (242-2450), Ozaukee County Country Club.
- Waukesha Curling Club (542-4461).
- Hart Park, Wauwatosa (258-1248).
- Wauwatosa Curling Club (257-9775).

Fishing

Your favorite sporting goods store can often tell you what's biting and where. Our park lagoons have been stocked, some with trout and bullheads, and Lake Michigan has been stocked with salmon. Don't forget that licenses are required for anglers age 16 and older; however, licenses are issued free to anyone over age 65.

- DNR hot-spot hotline (799-1300).
- Licensing information and license-sale sites (278-4072).
- Caution: Contact the DNR for information on PCB levels in Lake Michigan fish.

Frisbee

Here's a different way to enjoy Frisbee. Test your skill at the newly-installed 18-hole Disc Golf Course in Brown Deer Park. Be sure to take a Frisbee for everyone. We've found this to be a great family activity.

Golf

In addition to the private clubs, the Milwaukee County parks offer 16 golf courses. Golf reservations can be made by telephone at the individual county course. See the "County Parks at a Glance" chart in Chapter 3. You must have a Milwaukee County golf identification card, which can be picked up at Brown Deer, Currie, Grant, or Greenfield golf clubhouses for $5.00.

- Complete rate schedule (278-4345).

Gymnastics

Most YMCA's, the Jewish Community Center, and area recreation departments offer gymnastics classes. Especially well-known is the Milwaukee Turners School of Gymnastics (272-1844).

Hiking/Walking

From flowered boulevards to wooded parks and trails, most of Milwaukee invites exploration by foot. Some of our favorite city hikes are the Shorewood Nature Preserve, the Hawthorne Glen Nature Center in Wauwatosa, and the Schlitz Audubon Center. For great nature hikes outside the city, try Kettle Moraine State Park and Riveredge Nature Center (see Chapter 3). For those who want company, the Milwaukee Hiking Club and the Wisconsin-Go-Hikers organize treks to all kinds of interesting places. Look for announcements of their hikes and meeting places in the Accent Section of Friday's *Milwaukee Journal*. If you want to avoid the weather, try the shopping malls; they are often open early in the morning to encourage walkers. For more suggestions, see "Walking Tours" in Chapter 2.

- Jacobus Park Nature Trail (handicapped accessibility).
- Senior Citizens: Wisconsin-Go-Hikers offer midweek hikes.

Horseback Riding

A bridle path runs through Root River Parkway near Whitnall Park. Parkway Stables (425-1250) rents horses and offers lessons.

Hunting

Information concerning what game is in season, license fees, firearms regulations, and hunting sites may be obtained from the Department of Natural Resources (562-9500).

Ice Skating

You can find skating facilities ranging from simple to sophisticated. All the Milwaukee County park lagoons are delightful for skating. In addition, skating rinks are made in many of the parks; sites vary from year to year, but all are free and have warming houses with restrooms. Many municipalities have skating rinks; inquire at your local recreation department about locations and lessons.

Hart Park
7300 Chestnut, Wauwatosa (258-1248).
- Indoor rink.
- Wisconsin Curling Club.
- Open the weekend before Christmas and Sundays in January.
- Admission, free to Wauwatosa residents.

Mayfair Mall Ice Chalet
2300 North Mayfair Road, Wauwatosa (257-3111).
- Indoor rink, skate rental, summer classes.
- Ice Skating Institute of America; U.S. Figure Skating Association.
- Admission, fee.

Wilson Park
4001 South 20th Street, Milwaukee (281-4610).
• Indoor rink, open year-round.
• Greater Milwaukee Figure Skating Club.
• Admission, fee.

Wisconsin State Fair Park
Corner of 84th Street and Greenfield Avenue, West Allis.
• Olympic-sized speed-skating rink (476-3068).
• Indoor skating rink (257-8894).
• Wisconsin Figure Skating Club (257-2883).

Kite Flying

Let your imagination soar! If you've never flown or made a kite, you're missing some good fun. Workshops are taught by the Kite Society at the Milwaukee Public Museum from time to time. With kite in hand, head for the Lakefront. Or join the organized "fly-ins" (held May through September) co-sponsored by the Milwaukee County Park System and the Wisconsin Kite Society (562-8014). It's great fun!

Roller Skating

Skate along the Lakefront. Look for the skate rental concession vans on the McKinley Marina landfill. See the Yellow Pages for indoor rinks.

Rugby

• Milwaukee Men's Rugby Club (276-2677).
  P.O. Box 158, Milwaukee 53201.
• Milwaukee Women's Rugby Football Club (761-0786).
  3114 West Franklin Terrace, Franklin 53132.

Running/Jogging

The Badgerland Striders (548-0391) coordinates over 500 runs each year. Their newsletter is mailed to members and is available in running stores. Here is a small listing of some of our favorite runs:

• Al's Run, Sponsored by *The Milwaukee Journal*, September, 5 miles.
• Bonne Bell Run, for women only, May, 6.2 miles.
• Dinosaur Dash, sponsored by the Milwaukee County Public Museum, April, 3.1 miles.
• Gimbel's/M.A.C.C. Fund Run, sponsored by Gimbel's, June, 5 miles.
• Hoan Bridge (Nancy's favorite bridge) Run, sponsored by Milwaukee County Department of Parks, Recreation and Culture, August, 5 miles.
• Lite Beer Lakefront Marathon, Fall, 27 miles (from Grafton to the War Memorial).
• Run For Your Heart, sponsored by the Jewish Community Center (276-0716).
• Samson's Stomp, sponsored by the Milwaukee County Zoo, January, 6 miles.
• Stroh's Run, to help fund renovation of the Statue of Liberty, October.
• Super Run, to raise money for America's parks, June, 2 and 6 miles.

Sailing

Would you like to become a sailor? We were amazed to learn how simple it is. There is easy access to lessons, rentals, and launching sites at the Lakefront; the cost is affordable. Marquette University and UW-M have sailing clubs. See also the boat launching listings in the "County Parks at a Glance" chart in Chapter 3.

Milwaukee Community Sailing Center
1450 North Lincoln Memorial Drive (277-9094).
East of the lagoon on the Lakefront.
• Reasonable membership fee includes lessons.

Milwaukee Yacht Club
McKinley Marina (271-4455).
• Inexpensive lessons.

Sailing Charters
Admirals Wharf, South Water Street at Erie Street (228-8817).

Skiing

Comprehensive information for Wisconsin is available without charge from the Wisconsin Division of Tourism, P.O. Box 7606, Madison, Wisconsin 53707 (608/266-2161, toll free 800/362-9566). Ask for the booklet "Wisconsin: Winter Escape." It's terrific!

Cross-Country. We've found some of our favorite trails at the Schlitz Audubon Center, Lake Park, Whitnall Park, and the Milwaukee County Zoo. If you're new at this, you can even rent skis for the day at the Zoo or test your skill in one of the county parks. See the "County Parks at a Glance" chart in Chapter 3. The Snow Star Ski Club (258-1085, 543-4171) offers lessons in six county parks.

The "in" event for cross-country enthusiasts is the Birkebeiner, the famous 50-55 kilometer race held at Telemark, in northern Wisconsin, in February. Get in shape with the "Park-A-Beiner" held at Whitnall Park in January.

If you'd like company on the trails, contact the Nordic Ski Club of Milwaukee (242-2008), 100 South Highland, Thiensville 53092.

Downhill. Three Milwaukee County Parks have ski hills with tows. For current information and facility closing at the county sites, call 278-4343. See the Yellow Pages for commercial establishments and equipment rentals. Downhill ski clubs for adults are too numerous to mention; inquire at your favorite ski store for pamphlets and information, or write to Metropolitan Ski Council, P.O. Box 266, Milwaukee 53202.

Programs for children include transportation from city-wide pick-up points, lessons, and lift tickets:
- Blizzard Ski Club (762-1305)
  4860 South Austin Street, Oak Creek 53154.
- Snow Star Club (258-1085, 543-4171)
  8930 West North Avenue, Wauwatosa 53226.

Soccer

The **Wisconsin Soccer Association** (344-0380), 1428 North 27th Street, is open Monday-Friday 6-9pm, Saturday 9am-noon. President Mike Kabanica tells us that they coordinate 46 adult and 700 youth teams in the Milwaukee area; 15,000 kids register each year for this popular sport. Instruction and leagues are provided for all members. The Milwaukee Kickers are affiliated with this association. Sign up in late spring for the fall season; fee includes uniforms.

Swimming

Lake Michigan
The obvious place to swim is in Lake Michigan. For the hardy, the season begins when it's warm enough to take off your shirt. It's exhilarating, but be prepared: The mid-summer water temperature is usually in the 50s and 60s, and the wind is a factor.

See the "County Parks at a Glance" chart in Chapter 3 for the location of pools and Lake Michigan beaches. We have found two beautiful sandy beaches on Lake Michigan that are 45-50 miles north of Milwaukee. Take a picnic and go for the day.

- Harrington Beach State Park
  I-43 north to County Trunk D east; between Port Washington and Cedar Grove.

  On summer weekends and holidays take the shuttle bus from your car to the different park areas. The beach is beautiful. No lifeguards. Fee.

- Kohler-Andrae State Park
  I-43 north to Highway KK; 7 miles south of Sheboygan.

  There are 1½ miles of spectacular Lake Michigan beach in this 760-acre park. Picnic in the sand dunes. Fee.

Inland Lakes

- Firemans Park, Elkhart Lake
  On Highway A.
  A beautiful glacial lake at the north end of Kettle Moraine State Park. It's a quiet lake with a sandy bottom. Fee.

- Mauthe Lake, Fond du Lac County
  Highway 45 to Kewaskum; Highway 28 East to County Trunk S; north on GGG; north, again, to the park. 50 miles north of Milwaukee in the northern unit of Kettle Moraine State Park.
  May be full on a warm weekend (300-car capacity). Lifeguards and bathhouses. Fee.

- Menomonie Park Lannon Quarry, Lannon
  Highway 41 to Highway 74; west to County Trunk V, then north on V. 15 miles northwest of Milwaukee.
  With a capacity of 1200, there are often waits at this popular park. Lifeguards and a bathhouse. Fee.

- Mukwonago Park, Mukwonago
  Highway 15 southwest to Mukwonago; north on Highway 83, then west on Highway 99.
  This sandy-bottomed lake has lifeguards and a bathhouse. Fee.

- Quarry Lake Park, Racine
  Highway 31 south to Highway 38 southeast. 30 miles south of Milwaukee.
  Very clear, very warm and very sandy; great for kids and scuba divers. Life guards and changing rooms. Fee.

- Silver Lake Park, Kenosha
  I-94 south to Highway 50; west to County Trunk F, then south on F. 50 miles south of Milwaukee.
  Capacity crowds on warm weekends and even some weekdays. Large grassy picnic areas border the lake. Fee.

Tennis

See the "County Parks at a Glance" chart in Chapter 3.

Toboganning

See the "County Parks at a Glance" chart in Chapter 3.

Wind-Surfing

Join the flashiest craze on Lake Michigan. The Lakefront concession offers lessons, equipment, and rentals. Join the wind-surfers near the parking lot between Bradford Beach and the McKinley Marina. The Milwaukee Community Sailing Center (277-8576) guarantees to teach you to board-sail in six hours over a period of two days or your money back. Such a deal!

5
Entertainment

Milwaukee is an entertainment showcase, offering a variety of year-round events. Regular season performances of symphony, ballet, opera, and theater are supplemented by a number of national touring shows and ethnic, holiday, and summer festivals. Calendars of events and newsletters are often available for the asking. The Friday editions of *The Milwaukee Journal* and the *Sentinel,* the *Milwaukee Magazine,* and community newspapers are also good references for scheduled events and performances.

The Performing Arts Center is home for a number of nationally acclaimed fine-arts performing groups. In the summertime, watch for outdoor performances in the adjoining Peck Pavilion. The lovingly renovated Pabst Theater hosts a myriad of artistic performances. Don't overlook this theatrical jewel. The Lincoln Center for the Performing Arts is home base for resident artists and performers. These community-based groups emphasize innovation and experimentation. In the summertime, turn your attention to the Lakefront and to the Summerfest grounds.

Box Offices

Commercial
Alpine Valley Music Theatre, East Troy	1-800-342-3722
Fireside Playhouse, Fort Atkinson	1-563-9505
Greater Milwaukee Funline	799-1177
Lincoln Center for the Arts	272-2787
MECCA	271-7230
Melody Top Tent Theatre	353-7700
Pabst Theater	271-3773
Performing Arts Center	273-7206
Skylight Comic Opera Ltd.	271-8815
State Fair Park	257-8800
Sunset Playhouse	782-4430
Ticketcharge	799-1007
Ticketron	273-6400

College
The college campuses offer theatrical performances, children's theater, films, concerts, lectures, exhibits, and dance.

Alverno College	671-5482
Cardinal Stritch College	352-5400 ext. 291
Carroll College	547-1211
	547-5855 (after 4 pm)
Concordia College	344-3400
Marquette University	
Evan P. and Marion Helfaer Theatre	224-7504
Mount Mary College	258-5934
University of Wisconsin-Milwaukee	
Events Information	963-5900
Fine Arts	963-4308
Film Information (Evenings, Wednesday-Saturday)	963-7703
University of Wisconsin-Waukesha	544-8825
Wisconsin Conservatory of Music	276-4350

Ethnic Festivals

Ethnic hospitality is what Milwaukee is all about. The festivals are always in season. Celebrate! There are a zillion "Strawberry Fairs," church bazaars, and county fairs, too numerous to mention. Be sure to check *The Journal, Sentinel,* community newspapers, and *Milwaukee Magazine* for dates and places.

Entrance fees vary, although a few festivals are free. You can take advantage of reduced admission fees for fests held on the Summerfest grounds by watching for promotional coupons in the newspapers and at local merchants. There are "free admission" times for specific groups, including children under age 12. All of the fests can be an affordable family activity if you plan ahead.

The events listed here are month by month in the order that they occur, beginning in June.

June

Juneteenth Day
• Mid-June.
• Admission, free.

Thousands of celebrants jam North Third Street to celebrate the date in 1865 when slaves in Texas and Oklahoma learned of the Emancipation Proclamation.

Lakefront Festival of the Arts
• Mid-June.

See "Art Museum-Milwaukee" in Chapter 1 and this Chapter.

City of Festivals Parade
• Late June.

Milwaukee's fabulous festival season officially opens with this parade. It's a toe-tapping time as band after band marches east along Wisconsin Avenue to the Summerfest grounds. This is a unique parade, with elaborately decorated floats, and all of Milwaukee's colorfully costumed ethnic groups proudly dancing their way along the parade route. It's a real sight!

Summerfest
- Late June.
- Admission, fee.

This festival, lasting 12 delightful days, has earned its reputation as a real Milwaukee crowd pleaser. You can find all ages in the crowd, from toddlers to seniors. Some come for the music: 10 different stages feature jazz, rock, pop, bluegrass, classical, folk and more. Others come for the food served by Milwaukee's well-known restaurateurs. From appetizers to desserts, it's an ethnic eating treat.

A real plus for families is the number of well-planned activities for children; it's easy to spend the entire day. As you enter the grounds be sure to request a program guide so you can organize your time around the lively scheduled entertainment. Besides a 3-ring circus, there's a specially constructed theater with puppet and magic shows. The play area is one of the best in the city; it's a multilevel climbing extravaganza. A welcome addition is the sporting area. We watched everything from aerobics to the double-dutch jump-rope contest and the audience loved it all.

The crowds are enormous but there still seems to be room for strolling about. The main stage attractions, however, have long lines. The grandstand fills up early and fast. You can beat the parking congestion by catching the Summerfest shuttle (only 25¢ a ride) on Wisconsin Avenue.

July

Greek Festivals
- July (the weekend after the 4th).
- Admission, free.

The first festival is held at the Annunciation Greek Orthodox church, 9400 West Congress. All the goodies are made by church members. If you ever wanted to taste homemade Greek food, this is your opportunity: You can sample gyros, baklava, dolmades and spanakopitta. The church building was designed by Frank Lloyd Wright, so take some time to tour it as you enjoy the festivities.

A smaller Greek celebration is held at Sts. Constantine and Helen church, 2160 Wauwatosa Avenue, also in July.

King Richard's Faire
See Chapter 8.

Volkfest
- Mid-July.

The German Societies of Milwaukee celebrate at Old Heidelberg Park in Glendale.

La Kermesse de la Bastille
- Mid-July, to coincide with Bastille Day.
- Admission, free.

East Town goes "Left Bank"! Experience a variety of things French: crepes, fromages, cafes, patisseries, croissants and quiche. Munch and mingle. The distractions are plentiful — jugglers, mimes, waiter/waitress races, big bands, little bands, French chefs, sidewalk cafes, and bicycle races, and, for runners, something special: Storm the Bastille at midnight!

Great Circus Parade
• Mid-July, Sunday 2pm.

Hold your horses, here come the elephants! The greatest circus parade ever staged returns to the streets of downtown Milwaukee. This authentically recreated parade will feature over 500 draught horses pulling 75 intricately carved antique circus wagons, some with wild animals. The wagons are from Wisconsin's famed Circus World Museum at Baraboo.

Watch the steam train unload its precious cargo of circus wagons on Thursday afternoon at the lakefront Coach Yards. View the wagons and menagerie for free on Friday and Saturday, and attend the Carson & Barnes Circus, the largest show in the world performing under canvas, all at the Coach Yards.

Festa Italiana
• Mid-July.
• Admission, fee.

Real Third Ward nostalgia! Follow the procession from the Summerfest grounds to the former site of the "Little Pink Church" (Our Lady of Pompeii) after the noon Mass on Sunday. Opening night is Venetian, with a parade of lighted boats on Lake Michigan. This is a festival to eat at, so plan to arrive there with a big appetite. We sampled it all: sausage, spedini, lasagna, cannoli, spumoni and granita. The display of Italian wares is an additional treat. This Festa claims to be the largest Italian celebration in the United States. Organizers work closely with the Italian government to bring to Milwaukee fine entertainment with an old-world flavor.

German Fest
• Late July.
• Admission, fee.

"Slap dance," oompah bands, and famous Milwaukee Gemütlichkeit! Enjoy the crowd and sip the brew. Members and friends of the German-American societies prepare and serve German and continental treats, including delicious spanferkel (roast pig on a spit). Don't miss the cultural exhibits, including an elegant display of fine German glassware.

Jewish Jubilee
• Late July.
• Admission, free.

Nosh a knish and mingle at this giant block party. Celebrate at the Jewish Community Center, 1400 North Prospect Avenue. Every year, members of the community write and perform an original musical for their Jubilee. The production is always a sellout, so buy your tickets early.

August

Wisconsin State Fair
At the State Fair Park (257-8800).
Between 77th and 84th streets at Greenfield Avenue; exit I-94 at 84th Street.

- Early August (11 days).
- Admission, fee.

Here's a way for city folks to "go country." The Wisconsin State Fair offers a close-up view of squealing pigs, prize-winning bulls, furry rabbits and stomping Clydesdales. The animals are the big draw. Nine hundred thousand visitors can't be wrong. This is the place to be! Catch the Blue Ribbon Livestock Auction in the Coliseum where those in the know gather to see prize cattle, swine and sheep go to the highest bidder. The U.S. Grand National Truck and Tractor Pull Championship also draws a heavy crowd. There's entertainment on 17 stages plus top-name performers in the Grandstand. (An additional event fee is required for the Grandstand.) There are competitions for just about everything: Besides the best apple pie, patchwork quilt or Guernsey cow, how about the best Freckled Face, the best Funny Face or the best-matched set of twins? You don't have to go hungry at the fair, either. It's a Wisconsin tradition not to leave before you've tasted roasted corn-on-the-cob dipped in melted butter and sampled a freshly baked cream puff.

Gates open at 8am, buildings at 9am, but come early in the day; after 2pm parking can become a problem on beautiful summer days. RV camping facilities are available, but there are only 88 sites so reserve early.

▶ Special feature: Watch for ways to trim admission fees. There are newspaper coupons for opening day and carload admission days. Children age 11 and younger are admitted free. Handicapped persons are admitted for a reduced rate. Group discounts are available when ordering 35 or more tickets. Call the Special Events Department (257-8816).

Afro Fest
- Mid-August.
- Admission, fee.

The Black community welcomes you to experience its heritage. Dance groups, dressed in a flashing array of color, come to perform from various African countries, Jamaica, and the West Indies. Everyone loves the jazz, soul, rock, and reggae rhythms, but that's just the beginning. There is an entire African village set up on the Summerfest grounds. (Our kids were intrigued with this display.) Sample the barbecue, soul food, and rice patties; they're delicious. Area church choirs bring their gospel music to the Lakefront on Sunday.

Irish Fest
• Mid-August.
• Admission, fee.

The food is fresh, hearty and wholesome: potatoes, soda bread, stew and corned beef. But there's more than just good food at this festival. Celi dancing is demonstrated and taught early in the evening; try it. You'll also find traditional musicians playing Bohrud drums, blowing Uheillean pipes and singing rebel songs. A highlight is the Sunday Mass with the priests entering in procession led by a piper playing "Amazing Grace."

Fiesta Mexicana
• Late August.
• Admission, fee.

Sample a chimichunga while you watch hearty souls compete in the Jalapeno Pepper-Eating Contest. This fiesta has a distinctive taste all its own. There are mariachi bands, and the main stage features entertainers from Texas and Mexico. On Sunday, an outdoor Mass is celebrated in Spanish.

September

Polish Fest
• Early September.
• Admission, fee.

From the Polka Contest to the Sunday noon Mass at the Summerfest main stage, there's plenty of variety. The music is distinctly Polish and every region seems to have its own dance. The Gorale, Mazur, Sryrena, Polish Falcon Nest, and Wesoly Lud dance troupes are lively and colorfully costumed. Be adventurous. Sample a pierogi or a kielbasa (sausage), or some czarnina (duck blood soup) or chlodnik (chilled beet-and-cucumber soup with crabmeat). All the Polish fare is prepared by members of the Polish community. For dessert, there's Beggar's Cake, which is three feet long and cooked on a spit over an open fire. For the less daring, there are the standard Summerfest grounds vendors.

Oktoberfest
• September.

There are a number of Oktoberfests celebrated all over Wisconsin. These fests are famous for folk dancing, brass bands, bratwurst, spanferkel and sauerkraut. One of the largest in the Milwaukee area is at Old Heidelberg Park, 700 West Lexington Boulevard in Glendale.

November

Holiday Folk Fair
MECCA, 500 West Kilbourn Avenue (271-4000).

- November, the weekend before Thanksgiving.
- Admission, fee.
- Park in the Municipal Parking Lot or area commercial lots.
- Handicapped accessibility.

Milwaukee's great show of ethnic pride has been sponsored by the Pabst Brewing Company, the International Institute and more than 50 nationality groups. The real stars of this colorful event are your neighbors, costumed volunteers from many of those 50 ethnic groups. Stop by to chat with them as they enthusiastically serve up their native home-cooked delights. Catch the excitement on stage as group after group performs traditional dances. Sooner or later, the aromas in the air will lead you to the Sidewalk Cafe. Folks who come this way aren't afraid to indulge their palates. It's not uncommon to see people try venison, shish kebob, fellafel and Vietnamese egg rolls all in one meal, then top it off with mazurki, dobos torte and baklava for dessert.

You'll want to stop at the World Mart, which showcases artifacts, crafts and daily life of the ethnic groups featured in the cultural exhibits. It's a fine time to go shopping. There are original handicrafted items reasonably priced which make attractive gifts. Ask questions and mingle in the crowd. Have your name printed in Pakistani, chat with a Chinese acupuncturist or watch the seemingly effortless work of a Belgian lace-maker. Each year, different displays are designed to arouse your curiosity.

The Holiday Folk Fair traditionally honors a particular group during the festivities. Guest artists representing that country are invited to perform. A Young People's Matinee features tots-to-teens folk-dancing groups. If the urge to dance is too much for you to resist, you can join in the folk dancing at the beer garden in Old Pabst Park.

Call the International Institute (933-0521) to request the complete schedule of events. You can get times, prices, descriptions, and coupons for reserved seating.

Kids' Fest
MECCA, 500 West Kilbourn Avenue (271-4000).

- November, call to confirm this year's date.
- Admission, free.
- Park in the Municipal Parking Lot or area commercial lots.
- Handicapped accessibility.

Clowns, magic, and balloons delight the young crowd. Small ballerinas perform on four stages. The focus is on education, but it's all great fun. Find out about stranger awareness, Mr. Yuk, and street safety. Our kids even lined up to have the dentist check their teeth!

Downtown Christmas Parade
Held the Saturday before Thanksgiving, on Wisconsin Avenue. Sparkling events usher in the holiday season. Here are just a few of our other favorites.

December

Sing-It-Yourself *Messiah*
929 North Water Street (273-7121).

Sing with the Milwaukee Symphony Orchestra. Get free tickets at the First Wisconsin-Milwaukee banks.

TubaChristmas
929 North Water Street (273-7121).

Listen to the invigorating sounds of the Tuba Choir playing traditional and contemporary holiday music. Just imagine more than 20 Santa Clauses on stage, each toting a tuba, and children laughing and singing with delight.

A Christmas Carol
144 East Wells Street (271-3773).

Produced by the Milwaukee Repertory Theatre. A Milwaukee tradition that's a sellout each year. If you have a talented child, watch for the open tryouts.

The Nutcracker
See "Milwaukee Ballet" in Chapter 5.

Pabst Mansion
See Chapter 1.

Old-World Third Street
Wander through a restored 1880s neighborhood of import emporiums and specialty shops.

Music

Instrumental Music

Alpine Valley Music Theatre
Highway D, East Troy (414/642-3945).

- Summer outdoor performances.
- Admission, fee.
- People ages 16-86 will find a program to their tastes.

Artists Series at the Pabst
144 East Wells Street (271-4747, recorded message 271-3773).

- Performances October-April.
- Renowned classical artists and chamber music groups.

Musicians and music lovers sit side by side enjoying these memorable performances.

Chicago Symphony Orchestra
929 North Water Street (271-3101).

- The Milwaukee Series offers ten concerts on Monday evenings October-May.
- Tickets available for entire series or individual performances.

Civic Music Association
1630 East Royall Place (276-0615).
Office in the Charles Allis Art Museum.

A calendar of musical events is mailed to members. It's also available at *The Milwaukee Journal* Public Service Desk and the Milwaukee Public Libraries.

Miller Highlife Summer Concerts
- Performances held rain or shine July-August at the Milwaukee County Zoo and the Alpine Valley Music Theatre.
- Call Ticketron (273-6400) for performance schedule and ticket prices.

You can watch these performances from under the tent or on the lawn. Either way, the variety of these concerts pleases all tastes from symphony to rock, country to jazz. If you're headed for the Zoo, bring a picnic.

Milwaukee Catholic Symphony Orchestra
(671-4996).

- Performance times vary.
- Admission varies.

Milwaukee Chamber Orchestra
(273-7121).

- Performance times vary.
- Admission varies.

Milwaukee String Players Orchestra
- Watch for their appearances at Villa Terrace; performance times vary.

Milwaukee Symphony Orchestra
212 West Wisconsin Avenue (291-6000).

- Lukas Foss, conductor.
- Regular concert series are performed September-June on Thursday mornings at 11am (fashion show and coffee before), Friday and Saturday evenings at 8pm, and Sunday evenings at 7:30pm in Uihlein Hall of the Performing Arts Center.
- Season tickets go on sale in April for new subscribers; individual seats are available after September 1.
- Parking is available in the PAC structure (coupon books may be purchased) or in other commercial lots in the area.
- The Symphony is well-equipped for the hearing or visually impaired. Special seating and Braille or taped program notes are available upon request.

The Milwaukee Symphony Orchestra presents a fine selection of programs. Internationally known guest artists and conductors appear with the orchestra. There are well-rounded classical series, a pops series and two Sunday afternoon Kinderkonzerts. You can enjoy the Symphony at other sites during the year: Follow the orchestra to the Milwaukee County Zoo, the Summerfest grounds and even Carnegie Hall.

Music for Youth
929 North Water Street (272-8540).

- Performance times vary.
- Admission varies.

City-wide young people's orchestra program.

Music Under the Stars
- Summertime performances in the Washington Park Temple of Music and at Humboldt Park, sponsored by the Journal Company.
- Call for performance schedule (278-4389 9am-4pm weekdays).
- Admission is free, but tickets are required; watch for the coupons in the newspapers or pick them up at *The Milwaukee Journal* Public Service Desk. Seating is reserved, but the free tickets are also available before each performance.
- Call for information about other summer events at these sites (276-4350, 278-4389).

Summer evenings of music, all free! Watch the newspapers for programs, times, dates, and specific locations. Past schedules have included the Polish Mazur Dancers, barbershop quartets, and *Fiddler On the Roof*.

Newberry Brass Quintet
(273-7121).

- Performance times and places vary.
- Admission prices vary.

Performing Arts Center (PAC)
929 North Water Street (executive offices and general information 273-7121, box office 273-7206).

The splendid halls of the PAC are the scene of many musical happenings throughout the year. In addition to the seasons of resident companies, guest artists from all over the world provide musical experiences. Tickets may be ordered by telephone using a major credit card. Call for the monthly calendar of events.

Rainbow Summer at the PAC
See "Lunchtime Diversions," below.

Ravinia Music Festival
Box 896, Highland Park, Illinois 60035 (312/782-9696).
Edens Expressway to Lake-Cook Road, exit east.

* Summer outdoor performances June-September.
* Admission fees vary; under-the-roof and under-the-stars seating.

Ravinia is the home of the Chicago Symphony Orchestra during the summer months. In addition to the orchestra's fine performances, you can enjoy famous guest artists performing everything from the classics to jazz.

We're not sure which is more fun — hearing a star performance or indulging in an elaborately appointed picnic supper. It's a pleasure to relax in this beautiful setting. And for your picnic, don't be afraid to outdo yourself; it seems that elegance is always the fashion here. So, have fun and bring all you've got!

Sinfonia Concertante
(783-0318).

* Performance schedule varies.

Summer Concerts at St. Paul's
914 East Knapp Street (276-6277).

* Musicians in informal recitals at St. Paul's Episcopal church.
* Admission, free.

Summer Evenings of Jewish Music
1400 North Prospect Avenue (276-0716).

* A series of evening concerts performed at the Jewish Community Center.
* Admission, member and nonmember fees.

University of Wisconsin-Milwaukee
(Fine Arts Box Office 963-4308).

The Fine Arts Department sponsors musical events year-round including performances of the Woodwinds Arts Quintet, Fine Arts Quartet, Wind Ensemble and Symphony Band, Jazz Ensemble, Symphony Orchestra, faculty recitals, and opera.

UW-M Fine Arts Quartet
(Fine Arts Box Office 963-4308).

* Performs in the Fine Arts Recital Hall at UW-M.

This internationally acclaimed quartet displays its astonishing virtuosity year-round. Vacation with their "Summer Evenings of Music."

Waukesha Symphony Orchestra
(414/547-1858).
- Performances in Shattuck Auditorium on the Carroll College campus.
- Schedule varies; 4 Tuesday evening concerts between September and May.

Wauwatosa Community Concert Association
(453-1293).
- Performances in the Wauwatosa East High School.
- Guest artist series; 4 concerts between September and May.

Wisconsin Conservatory of Music
1584 North Prospect Avenue (276-5760).
- Faculty and student recitals throughout the year. The public is invited to attend.

Vocal Music

These groups perform at various times throughout the year. Call for their schedules and watch for their performances around the community. Their tryouts are often announced in the newspapers.

Bel Canto Chorus	276-8533
Florentine Opera	273-1474
Juneautown Opera	464-6779
Milwaukee Choristers	271-7434
Milwaukee Opera	272-2787, 962-7050
Skylight Comic Opera Ltd.	271-8815
Wisconsin Conservatory of Music	276-5760

    Chamber Singers
    Children's Chorus
    Singers
    Symphony Chorus
    Vocal Arts Consort

Theater

Broadway Troupes and Star Performers

Melody Top Tent Theatre
7201 West Good Hope Road.

- Ticket information 353-7700.
- Season June-September.

Riverside Theatre
116 West Wisconsin Avenue.

- Ticket information 271-2000.
- Traveling stars and Broadway shows appear year-round in this ornate, newly decorated movie palace.

Spotlight Series/Edgewood Agency
- Ticket information 276-4544.
- Performances at the Performing Arts Center and the Pabst Theater.
- Tickets for individual productions may be purchased at the box office.

Children's Theater

Great American Children's Theater
- Ticket information 276-3482.
- Performances at the Pabst Theater.

PAC Programming for Young People
929 North Water Street.

- Productions in spring and fall; call for schedule (273-7121).
- Performances at the Performing Arts Center in Uihlein and Vogel halls.
- National touring productions in all the performing arts for young people; past performances have included the National Tap Dance Company of Canada and *Pinocchio*, a puppet show.

Theatre School, Ltd.
- Ticket information 273-7121 ext. 336.
- Summer performances mid-June to mid-July, Tuesday-Saturday at the Children's Zoo.
- Performances scheduled in area public schools in conjunction with the Children's Division of the Milwaukee Public Library.
- Call for class schedules.

West Allis Players
- Ticket and schedule information 327-7168.
- One show per month October-February.
- Performances at Nathan Hale High School, in cooperation with the West Allis Recreation Department.

Community Theater

Be a star, work a crew, or be part of the audience. Community theaters invite your support and participation. Auditions are usually open to the public. Check *The Milwaukee Journal, Milwaukee Sentinel,* and community newspapers for ticket and production information. The season generally runs from fall to spring.

Brookfield Players
- Ticket and schedule information 771-6911.
- Performances at the Brookfield Central High School.

Greendale Suburban Players
- Ticket and schedule information in *The Milwaukee Journal.*
- Performances at Greendale High School and Intermediate School.

Milwaukee Players
- Ticket and schedule information 271-3773.
- Performances at the Pabst Theater.

Mukwonago Village Players
- Ticket and schedule information 414/363-7318.
- Performances at Mukwonago High School.

Oak Creek Community Theater
- Ticket and schedule information 764-2637.
- Performances at Oak Creek Senior High School Theater.

Shorewood Players
- Ticket and schedule information 332-6944.
- Performances at Shorewood Community Auditorium.

Sunset Playhouse
- Ticket and schedule information 782-4430.
- Performances at Sunset Playhouse, 800 Elm Grove Road, Elm Grove.
- Seven productions year-round.

Waukesha Civic Theater
- Ticket and schedule information 414/547-0708.
- Performances at the theater, 1506 North Washington Avenue, Waukesha.

Wauwatosa Players
- Ticket and schedule information in *The Milwaukee Journal.*
- Performances at the Children's Home Theater at the County Institutions grounds.

West Allis Players
- Ticket and schedule information 327-7168 and in *The Milwaukee Journal.*
- Performances at West Allis Central High School, 8615 West Lincoln Avenue.

Whitefish Bay Players
- Ticket and schedule information 963-3936.
- Performances at the Whitefish Bay High School Auditorium.

Dinner Theater

Dick Shore Dinner Theatre
11811 West Bluemound Road, in the Ramada Sands Hotel (291-9949 after 3 PM).
• Musical revues year-round.
• Luncheons on Thursday and Friday, dinners on Saturday.

Fireside Playhouse
Highway 26 South, Fort Atkinson (414/563-9505).
• Performances year-round; call for schedule and ticket information.

Local Companies

Acacia Theatre Company
2844 North Oakland Avenue (962-2380).
• Performances at the Eastbrook Center Theatre.

The troupe emphasizes Christian values in its selection of plays. Past seasons' performances have ranged from Shakespeare to *The Four Poster*. The company is also available for performances in churches.

Clavis Theatre Company
900 South Fifth Street (272-1340).
• Performances at the Enclave Theatre, Wednesday-Sunday evenings.

"Milwaukee's professional off-Broadway theatre company" is dedicated to presenting productions that might not otherwise get to Milwaukee.

Court Street Theatre
315 West Court Street (273-7121).
• Performances at the Court Street Theatre, February-May.

The second stage of the Milwaukee Repertory presents innovative, experimental works.

Friends Mime Theatre
820 East Knapp Street (272-2787).
• Performances in season at Lincoln Center for the Performing Arts; in summer, throughout Milwaukee.

This troupe incorporates mime and storytelling into original works.

Hansberry-Sands Theatre Company, Inc.
820 East Knapp Street (272-2787).
• Performance sites may vary; call in September for the schedule.

This semiprofessional company performs modern dramas from a Black perspective.

Milwaukee Repertory Theatre
929 North Water Street (273-7121).

- Performances at the Todd Wehr Theatre, the river entrance to the Performing Arts Center; Tuesday-Sunday.
- Season ticket sales begin April 1.
- Inquire about signed performances for the hearing impaired.

John Dillon is artistic director of this nationally acclaimed repertory theater. Single tickets are often difficult to get for these outstanding performances; consider season tickets.

Paradox Studio Theatre, Inc.
820 East Knapp Street (272-2787).

- Performances in Ivory Hall at Lincoln Center for the Performing Arts.

The season varies, but there is an on-going play-writing competition, with the winning entries put into production.

Perhift Yiddish Theatre
1400 North Prospect Avenue (276-0716).

- Performances at the Jewish Community Center; schedule varies.

This oldest continuously operating Yiddish theater in the United States is nationally known.

Theatre X
820 East Knapp Street (272-2787).

- Performances at the Black Box Theatre at Lincoln Center for the Performing Arts; on tour for half the season.

This experimental theatre has a special interest in producing new works.

The Rest

Dance

Folk Dancing
Folk dancing has lots of followers in Milwaukee. Clubs from many nationalities meet and dance throughout the year. Call the International Institute (933-0521) for a listing of specific club contacts. Some groups announce their activities in the newspapers. And don't forget to see the Holiday Folk Fair (see "Ethnic Festivals" in this chapter).

Lincoln Center for the Performing Arts
820 East Knapp Street (272-2787).

- Bauer Dance Company
- Dancecircus
- J.U.M.P. Dance Theatre

All three groups are headquartered here. Performance schedules and admission prices vary.

Ko Thi Dance
(933-7007).

- Performance schedules and prices vary.

This 15-year-old Black dance troupe performs and offers classes.

Milwaukee Ballet Company
504 West National Avenue (643-7677).

- Ted Kivitt, artistic director.
- Performances at the Performing Arts Center (box office 273-7206) October-May.
- Spring brochure announces programs, series offerings, and premier works.
- Series tickets go on sale in the spring; individual tickets may be available later. Check at the PAC box office.

A ballet company to watch; each season sees an increased repertoire of classical and contemporary works. The talented members of this troupe contribute original choreography throughout the season. The costumes and sets for the annual performances of "The Nutcracker" (December) are enchanting. This is a sellout every year so buy your tickets early for this traditional treat.

Film Revivals & Series

Art Museum — Milwaukee
750 North Lincoln Memorial Drive (271-9508).

There are separate film series scheduled for weekends, including Reel Art, Film (visual and performing art), and the latest series for children.

Discovery and Travel Series (sponsored by the Milwaukee Public Museum)
1015 North 6th Street (278-2748).

- Programs held in Cooley Hall at M.A.T.C.
- Fall-spring; 16 programs, Sundays at 2:30pm.
- Admission, fee.

Gallery Cinema
2901 South Delaware Avenue (481-3004).

- Admission, fee.

Revival films presented by Milwaukee Film Classics, with an introduction to each film. Call for times and titles.

Milwaukee Public Museum
Saturday Film Series.
800 West Wells Street (278-2727).

- Shown in the Lecture Hall on the main floor.
- Fall-spring, 16 films, Saturday afternoons.
- Admission, fee.

Also see "Lunchtime Diversions" in this chapter.

Oriental Landmark Theatre
2230 North Farwell Avenue (276-8711).

Catch a double or triple feature. Stay for the midnight "Rocky Horror Picture Show" if you can sit that long. (The springs in some seats are sprung.)

Shorewood Travel and Adventure Series (sponsored by M.A.T.C.)
1701 East Capitol Drive (962-2938, recorded message).

- Guest traveler and film series presented in the Shorewood Community Auditorium.
- Begins last Sunday in January; 12 programs, Sunday afternoons.
- Admission, fee.

University of Wisconsin-Milwaukee
- Current and revival films at various campus locations. Call for times and places (963-7703 evenings, Wednesday-Saturday).
- Kinder Cinema — films for children. Sunday afternoons September-May. Admission 95¢. Call for schedule (963-4825).

Lunchtime Diversions

Brown Bach It
929 North Water Street (273-7121).

- In Mangin Lounge at the Performing Arts Center.
- April and October, Tuesdays and Thursdays.
- Free concerts by local artists.

The most relaxing lunchtime atmosphere we know.

Jazzy Lunches
750 North Lincoln Memorial Drive (271-9508).

- Outdoors on the Lincoln Memorial Bridge at the Milwaukee Art Museum.
- June through August, Fridays.
- Free music: folk, jazz and contemporary. Food and beverages may be purchased. Cancelled when it rains.

Tell your friends to meet you on the bridge.

Karl Zeidler Park
301 West Michigan Street (278-4389).

- July and August, Tuesdays and Thursdays at 11:30am.
- Free band concerts. Schedules may vary; extra concerts added without notice. Held in the bandstand. (A touch of nostalgia.)

Milwaukee Public Museum
800 West Wells Street (278-2700).

- "Brown Bag Film Series"; each year a different theme is selected for this series. Watch for it in March.

Rainbow Summer at the PAC
929 North Water Street (273-7121).

- Sponsored by the Journal Company in the Peck Pavilion at the Performing Arts Center.
- July through August weekdays.
- Free performances in all the performing arts from Balkan Band to mime, jazz, poetry and classical music.

Not just for people working downtown, this is a great lunchtime treat for kids. Check newspapers for specific performance schedules.

University of Wisconsin-Milwaukee

3200 North Downer Avenue (963-1122 7:15am-4:30pm).

This campus is a resource for the whole community. Call 963-5538 or 963-6628 for "Preview: A Calendar of Events," a comprehensive and well-designed program guide. A small sample of campus offerings follows.

American Geographical Society Collection
2311 East Hartford Avenue (963-6282).

- Open weekdays 8am-5pm, Saturday 8am-noon.
- Admission, free.

A priceless collection of maps, old globes, atlases and charts, plus 180,000 books and 400,000 journals comprise this national treasure housed in the Golda Meir Library, third floor east wing.

Art Galleries
A calendar of programs, exhibits, and hours for the three following galleries is printed three times each year. Call to get on the mailing list (963-6509).

► Art History Gallery
  Room 154 Mitchell Hall, Kenwood Boulevard at Downer Avenue (963-4060).
► Fine Arts Galleries
  Fine Arts Center (963-4946).
► University Art Museum
  Vogel Hall, 3253 North Downer Avenue (963-6509).

Permanent exhibits include the Rogers Collection of Greek and Russian icons and the Rosenberg collection of modern European works of art.

The Craft Centre
Room EG30 UW-M Union (963-5535 after 1pm).

Noncredit courses for your enjoyment. Call for course offerings and registration.

College For Kids/High Interest Day (963-6364).
Gymnastics Class (963-6348).

These classes are designed and implemented by University faculty and community experts to allow short and enriching in-depth study not found in a traditional classroom. Geared for children K-8 with a high academic potential, these classes are held in summer and on Saturdays during the school year. Call to get brochures with class descriptions.

Elderhostel
(963-5038).

Classes are offered on this campus as part of a national program for senior citizens. Classes are also scheduled at Cardinal Stritch College and other UW campuses.

Greene Memorial Museum
See Chapter 1.

Olsen Planetarium
1900 East Kenwood Boulevard (963-4961 during the school year).

• Admission, fee.

Star shows for groups of up to 70 people are available for $25. Why not try it for your next party?

Science Bag Lectures
Room 137 Physics Building, Kenwood Boulevard at Cramer Street (963-4474).

Programs are conducted November-March, Fridays at 8pm. For interested non-scientists ages 8-80. These monthly programs, sponsored by the Physics Department, explore fascinating phenomena. Look for the tempting program titles in the "Preview: A Calendar of Events."

Union
2200 East Kenwood Boulevard (963-5900).

A variety of events and programs; call for the printed monthly schedule.

Wisconsin State Fair Park
Between 77th and 84th streets at Greenfield Avenue, West Allis 53214 (257-8800).

Events geared to your particular interest are scheduled throughout the entire year: dog shows, horse shows, Rummage-O-Rama, antiques shows, and a variety of races. Write or call (257-8800) for a complete calendar of events.

Tried It All?

At Wit's End?
When the kids tell you there's nothing to do, pile them into your car and drive through a local car wash. It's a change of pace which our kids love. If nothing else, your car will be clean.

Club Garibaldi
2501 South Superior Street (747-1007).

- Fridays 8-9:30pm.
- Admission, fee.

Join the folk dancing. Beginners and experts dance together.

Custard
Real Milwaukee flavor! We can't agree on which is best. These are some of our favorites. You be the judge.

Gilles Frozen Custard Drive-In
7515 West Bluemound Road (453-4875).

Kitt's Frozen Custard Drive-In
7000 West Capitol Drive (461-1400).

Kopp's Frozen Custard Stand
6005 West Appleton Avenue (873-3860).
7631 West Layton Avenue (282-4080).
5373 North Port Washington Road (961-2006).

The phone numbers are recorded special-flavor hotlines.

Leon's Frozen Custard Drive-In
3131 South 27th Street (383-1784).

Pig 'n' Whistle (in the back)
1111 East Capitol Drive (964-3450).

Embroiderers Guild of America (Badger Chapter)
1144 East Henry Clay (463-1918).

- Meets in the Henry Clay Elementary School; scheduled monthly meetings, membership required.
- Workshops, lectures, shows, and practice of any needle art.

Equestrian Events.
The horsey set and admirers meet at Wisconsin State Fair Park several times during the year. Look for the Wisconsin Arabian Horse Show (June), Wisconsin Quarter Horse Show (August), and the American Saddle Horse Show (September).

Milwaukee Chess Club
Enderis Playground — 2938 North 72nd Street (353-9080).
* Tuesday, 7:30pm.
* Admission, fee.

Polar Bear Swim
New Year's Day at Bradford Beach.
Q. How do you tell the swimmers from the icebergs?
A. The swimmers shiver.

Teatime
Try a traditional English teatime.
George Watts Tea Room
761 North Jefferson Street (276-6352).

Linden Room
Marshall Field and Company (771-2121).
2500 North Mayfair Road (in Mayfair Mall).

Timber Wolf Farm
6669 South 76th Street, one mile south of Southridge (425-8264).
* 10am-3pm, Saturday and Sunday.
* Admission, fee.

Yearling and adult timber wolves in an outdoor setting, presented by the Timber Wolf Preservation Society.

Wisconsin Skydivers/Parachute Club
W204 N5022 Lannon Road, Menomonee Falls (252-4319).
* Aero Park Airport.
* 18 years and older.
* 4-5 hour lesson, $85.00, includes one static-line jump, plane, and equipment. Qualified instructors.

Woodland Pattern Inc.
720 East Locust Street (263-5001).
* Open Tuesday-Friday noon-8pm, Saturday-Sunday noon-5pm; open one hour prior to readings and events.

This is not just a bookstore. Despite its appearance (8,000 books, hundreds of records and cassettes), it is a nonprofit, tax-exempt literary arts center dedicated to presenting literature, music, and performance by living artists. Call or stop in. They love to chat about their programs and services, and the enthusiasm is contagious!

6
Eclectic Shopping

The listings in this section have met the broad criterion of tickling our fancies. No attempt has been made to be comprehensive. If you have suggestions for entries in future editions, please drop us a line.

Great Groceries

Ambrosia Chocolate Factory Outlet Store
1133 North Fifth Street (271-2089).
Perfumes the downtown; fine chocolate and other treats.

Asian Mart
1107 North Third Street (765-9211).
For that change-of-pace menu.

Bagel Nosh Delicatessen
4170 North Oakland Avenue (961-0770).
Fresh bialys, pletzels, schlamalies, and, of course, bagels.

Balkan Trading Company
938 West Lapham Boulevard (643-7372).
Serbian specialty shop; smoked meats, burek, sour dough bread, and more.

Beans and Barley
1901 East North Avenue (278-0234).
Natural foods that everyone likes. Eat here or just buy the ingredients.

Bits of Britain
1201 East Russell Avenue (744-3989).
British foods and gifts.

Chocolate Swan Ltd.
890 Elm Grove Road (784-7926).
Homemade chocolate delicacies; truffles, handmade tinted white chocolate roses, and English toffee cake.

Coffee Trader
2625 North Downer Avenue (332-9690).
Good coffee and imported food selections. Check out the chocolates around the corner; they carry Neuhaus.

Empire Fish
11200 West Watertown Plank Road (259-1330).
Fresh fish from seven seas.

Foods of All Nations
4827 West North Avenue (871-5650).
Real goat's milk feta cheese.

Gibbsville Cheese Factory
Sheboygan Falls (414/564-3242).
45 minutes north of Milwaukee. Exit I-43 at Oostburg.
Worth a detour; the colby is a special treat.

Glorioso's Market
1020 East Brady (272-1311).
Mediterranean delights, not just Italian. The biggest olive oil selection we've found.

Herb Society of America Annual Plant Sale
Boerner Botanical Gardens in Whitnall Park; call for this year's date (425-1130).

Honey Acres
See Chapter 2.

Hong Fat Company
1112 North Third Street (273-1727).
Oriental grocery. Ask for their wonderful, fresh bean sprouts.

Indian Mart Inc.
4215 West North Avenue (444-5444).
For that change-of-pace menu.

Indian Groceries and Spices
4807 West North Avenue (445-9202).
Exotic flavors for your next meal.

Larry's Brown Deer Market
8737 North Deerwood Drive, Brown Deer (355-9650).
Oh, their "killer brownies," and everything for entertaining!

Mila's K and K Bake Shop
233 North Main Street, Thiensville (242-1404).
The Moscow rye bread is tops.

Mitchell Street Green Market
Mitchell Street at 13th (278-3674).
This is a seasonal outdoor market where local farmers sell anything grown in Wisconsin. 8am-sellout.

Niemann's Home Made Chocolate Shop
7475 Harwood Avenue, Wauwatosa (744-4940).
Charming chocolates, timeless atmosphere. Closed Monday.

Olympia Foods
4304 West Vliet Street (342-8899).
Imported Greek olives, olive oil, cheeses, coffee, tea, spices, filo, and Greek pastry.

Oriental Supreme Co. Inc.
6918 North Teutonia Avenue (351-4511).
For a change-of-pace menu, inquire about the free Chinese cooking demonstrations.

Outpost Natural Foods Co-op
3500 North Holton Street (961-2597).
Cheeses, grains, dried fruits, and nuts in bulk. A "gluten-free" shelf for the allergic.

Peter Sciortino Bakery
1101 East Brady Street (272-4623).
The crusts crunch on their delicious Italian bread.

Sendik's Markets
2643 North Downer Avenue (962-1600).
4027 North Oakland Avenue (332-3140).
530 East Silver Spring Drive (962-9525).
The exotic, the elegant, and the out-of-season in a tasteful environment.

Simma's Ovens Bakery
817 North 68th Street, Wauwatosa (257-0998).
World class desserts. To miss her chocolate truffles would be a sin.

The Spice House
1102 North Third Street (272-1888).
Your nose knows. Ask for their own private blends; they're great.

Sweet 'n' Counters
5900 North Port Washington Road, Bay Shore Mall (964-9546).
Diabetic, diatetic, delicious candies.

Sweet Sensations
4006 North Oakland Avenue (964-2466).
Fine chocolates locally made. Pastries from the Chocolate Swan — buy a whole, a half, a quarter, or just a slice.

Trade Winds Spice Ltd.
6507 West North Avenue, Wauwatosa (257-3368).
All the spices you'd expect plus those you've never heard of and will want to try. Delightful hand-mixed teas, spiced and herbal, and great dried vegetables.

Usinger's Sausage Store
1030 North Third Street (276-9100).
A double treat — sausage and German decor.

West Allis Farmer's Market
1559 South 65th Street, West Allis (476-3774).
• Tuesday, Thursday, Saturday; May 1-last weekend in November. No sales before 1pm.
If you can be there when it opens, you'll get the pick of the produce from asparagus to zucchini, everything produced on Wisconsin farms and picked, plucked, or gathered that morning: chicken, eggs, plants, produce, fresh flowers. Talk to the "honey man" about his bees.

Woelke-Schultze Market
3725 West North Avenue (444-2750).
Smoke the fish you caught or choose from their large selection of smoked foods.

Pick-Your-Own Produce

It is easy to find "pick your own" farms within 30 minutes of almost anywhere in Milwaukee. There's nothing better than popping a freshly picked berry into your mouth on a sunny June day or taking a bite from a crisp apple just pulled from the tree. The "Good Things To Eat" section of the classified ads in most papers lists seasonal fruits and vegetables as well as picking locations. You must call in advance because crop availability varies from day to day. Take your own bushel baskets or buy them at the farms. If you don't want to stoop or stretch, check the Farmers' Markets listings in this chapter. Here are our favorites:

Barthel Fruit Farm
12246 North Farmdale Road 99W, Mequon (242-2737).

We've had great experiences taking families and large groups to Barthel's. Picking in the fall is cool and pleasant. It's more than apples!

Green Meadows Farm
P.O. Box 182, Waterford 53185 (534-2891).
I-94 exit west Racine-Waterford; travel 18 miles on Highway 20.

The farm is 30 minutes southwest of Milwaukee. This makes a great October outing; pick a pumpkin and prepare for Halloween.

Bargains

Factory Outlets

Allen Edmonds Shoe Bank Bootery
775 Main Street, Belgium (285-3481).
Top-of-the-line men's shoes; especially convenient for the hard to fit.

Branovan Shoe Company
6555 West Mill Road (353-6900).
Dress and athletic shoes for men and women.

Brownberry Ovens
17365 Bluemound Road (784-0778).
Bakery goods.

Carter's
52nd Street in the K-Mart shopping center, Kenosha.
Cotton clothing for women and children; Jockey products for men.

Chocolate House
4121 South 35th Street (281-7803)
Bulk chocolate, candy, and fudge.

Dressing Down
6546 North 76th Street (353-0533).
Jansport running shorts, "sweats," T-shirts, and backpacks.

Everitt Knitting Mills
234 West Florida Street (276-4647).
Knitwear for women and children, piece goods.

Fiberesin
3703 East Wisconsin Avenue, Oconomowoc (567-9213).
• Open Tuesday-Saturday, 9am-5:30pm
Fiberboard furniture and shelving.

Junior House
710 South Third Street (744-5080).
Women's sportswear. Watch for their warehouse sales for piece goods and clothing. (Wear a leotard; there are no dressing rooms.) Classic styling, great values.

Knit Pikker
2942 South 108th Street, West Allis (327-7010).
Knit clothing and accessories.

Kuppenheimer
7690 West Appleton Avenue (463-6303).
2964 South 108th Street (543-8300).
Men's clothing, traditional styling.

Milwaukee Soap Company
1526 North 31st Street (342-5733).
5661 South 27th Street (282-7880).
Laundry and dish soap and bathroom tissue.

Mrs. Karl's Bakery
1923 West Pierce Street.
14680 West Greenfield Avenue.
6204 South Packard Avenue.
7970 North 76th Street.
Bakery goods.

Oster Company
5021 North Lydell Avenue (332-8300).
Small electrical appliances.

Pepperidge Farm Thrift Shop
3902 North 76th Street (461-0050).
Bakery goods.

Also Worth A Look

Burlington Coat Factory Warehouse
1501 West Jewel Court (764-2474).
6548 North 76th Street (358-0500).
Clothes, coats, and shoes for all ages; stock up on stockings.

Factory Outlet Center
I-94 and Highway 50, Kenosha. On the service road. Exit at Howard Johnson's Motor Lodge.
Thirty-four stores.

Kahn's Clothing
602 North Broadway Street (289-9470).
Men's clothing.

Loehmann's
10328 West Silver Spring Drive (464-8850).
Bluemound and Calhoun roads in Market Square.
Women's clothing; look for fabulous labels.

Park-It-Market
Milwaukee County Stadium (355-8371).
A grandddaddy of garage sales, with fresh produce and entertainment.

J.C. Penney
10332 West Silver Spring Drive (464-1111).
5656 South Packard Avenue, Cudahy (769-6210).
Catalogue overstocks and returns.

Sears, Roebuck and Company
▶ Appliances and Furniture Outlet
6001 West State Street (259-0905).
▶ Surplus Store
10635 West Greenfield Avenue (259-0033).

Browsing

Auctions
From glorious estates to backyard junk. Call for sale dates and ask to be added to their mailing lists. Regular auctions are held at:

Broadway Auction Gallery
513 North Broadway Street (276-3620).

Milwaukee Auction Gallery
4747 West Bradley Road (355-5054).

New Berlin Auction and Sales Barn
17655 West National Avenue (679-0780).

Travis Auction Galleries
1422 Underwood Avenue (453-0342).

Shopping Areas
To buy or not to buy is not the question. These places will occupy an hour or more just discovering what's there.

Cedar Creek Settlement
N70 W6340 Bridge Road, Cedarburg (377-8020).

Downer Avenue
Between East Webster and East Park streets.

Jefferson Street
Between Kilbourn and Clybourn streets.

Market Place
Highway 32 and Puetz Road, Oak Creek (762-1816).
• Closed Monday.

Old World Third Street
Between West Wells Street and West Highland Boulevard.
• Most shops closed Sunday.

Stonecroft
County Road C, town of Grafton (377-6150).
• Closed Monday.

Stonewood Village
17700 West Capitol Drive, Brookfield (781-9703).
• Closed Sunday.

Village of Wauwatosa
West State Street at Harwood Avenue.

Water Street
► Clothes Rack
203 North Water Street (224-4951).
Women's clothing.
► MELCO Clothing
200 South Water Street (273-6682).
Men's clothing.
► Mitchell Manufacturing
249 North Water Street (272-5942).
Leather jackets, handbags, and luggage.
► Odds 'n' Ends
231 East Chicago Street (272-5084).
• Open September-January.
Knitwear.
► Wisconsin Linen
200 South Water Street (224-6185).
Sheets, towels, comforters and table linens.

West Bend
► Amity/Enger-Kress Outlet Store
505 Rolfs Road (338-6506).
Small leather goods, known especially for their wallets.
► Explorers Shop
253 South Main Street.
Small leather goods.
► Factory Outlet Cookware
255 South Main Street.
Regal and Mirro cookware.
► West Bend Company Outlet Store
445 Western Avenue (334-2311).
• Open 9:30am-5pm weekdays, 9am-1pm Saturday.
Small electrical appliances, pots and pans.
► West Bend Factory Shopping Mall
At the Junction of Highways 45 and 33.
Sixteen stores. Finish munching your Ambrosia chocolate before you go to the Mountain Camper.

Shopping Malls

Our metropolitan shopping centers offer a wide variety of goods and services, from ice cream to ice skating. Store hours in general are Monday through Saturday, 9am-9pm, Sunday noon-5pm.

Bayshore
5900 North Port Washington Road (332-8136).

Brookfield Square
95 North Moorland Road (786-3430).

Capitol Court
5500 West Capitol Drive (837-8800).

Grand Avenue
161 West Wisconsin Avenue (224-0384)

Mayfair
2500 North Mayfair Road (771-1300).
• Indoor Ice Chalet (257-3111).

Northridge
7700 West Brown Deer Road (354-2900).

Point Loomis
3555 South 27th Street (780-7733).

Southgate
3333 South 27th Street (645-6928).

Southridge
5300 South 76th Street (421-1102).

Specialty Shops

American Science Center, Inc.
5430 West Layton Avenue (281-2322).
Gizmos and whizbangers. Wonderful junk you won't find anywhere else.

Arenz Cutlery
101 East Wells Street (272-2217).
A fine selection of German cutlery.

Art Supplies (beyond the tube and brush):
▶ Palette Shop
   342 North Water Street (272-3780).
   704 North Milwaukee Street (224-9720).
▶ Sax Art Supplies
   1101 North Third Street (272-1890).
▶ Tesseract
   4828 West Donges Bay Road, Thiensville (242-2940).
   Beads, crafts and needlework.

Bartz Displays Inc.
6931 West North Avenue (453-2553).
Party supplies for any theme; wild Halloween masks, but not for the faint-hearted!

Betty's Bead Bank
300 West Juneau Avenue (347-0730).
823 North Second Street (347-0434).
We can't imagine there is a bead they don't have. It's do-it-yourself jewelry and hours of entertainment for pennies.

Dick Dahlman's Antiques and Reproductions
10930 West Loomis Road, Franklin (761-1015).
One mile west of Highway 100.
Acres of stuff, from brass to clocks and almost everything in between. It's dusty fun, a knickknack heaven.

Easter Seal Society Shop
623 North Milwaukee Street (272-0378).
Hand-crafted items, including beautiful wooden toys, made by handicapped artisans.

George Watts and Son
761 North Jefferson Street (276-6352).
Elegant china, crystal and silver. A Milwaukee symbol of good taste.

Goldmann's Department Store
930 West Mitchell Street (645-9100).
Don't give up until you've tried Goldmann's. It's a legend!

Great Lakes Futons
1428 North Farwell Avenue (272-3324).
Japanese sleeping mats, wildly colorful kites and wind socks. Personalize your own kimono.

Laacke and Joys Company
1433 North Water Street (271-7878).
All the gear it takes to enjoy Wisconsin's weather.

Milwaukee Map Service
4519 West North Avenue (445-7361).
Plan a trip to anywhere; for the collector or the disoriented.

Milwaukee Sports Collector Store — Ballfour Cards
2844 West Forest Home Avenue (383-1280).
Bring in your cards, the older the better. Buy, sell, or trade baseball memorabilia.

Napoleon's
3948 North Maryland Avenue (962-6730).
War-gamers' supply center.

Renaissance Book Shop
834 North Plankinton Avenue (271-6850).
Also at the airport.
Five floors of secondhand books; if you can't find it here, you probably can't find it anywhere.

Restaurant Supplies
Everything from soup pots to nutcrackers.
- ▶ F.W. Boelter Restaurant Supplies
  1136 West National Avenue (645-2050).
- ▶ Fein's Restaurant Supply
  2007 North Third Street (562-0220).

Spheeris Sporting Goods
7201 West Capitol Drive (464-2800).
Fishing, hunting, and sporting goods — a lure for every fish.

TLC Toys
127 East Silver Spring (332-5769).
Toys, carefully chosen to stimulate imaginative play. Don't look here for the latest battery-operated gimmick. These toys are exquisite, expensive, and really fun.

7
Family Dining

The easiest way to eat out with children is quickly. That often leads to fast food — the shake-and-burger avenue — but everyone already knows that route. We've gone a bit further and listed a few restaurants we've found convenient for family outings. You'll find fish fries first, followed by restaurants arranged by area.

When you eat out in Milwaukee, you can sample culinary pleasures from many countries. We were overwhelmed by the variety and quality of restaurants in our city. We suggest you consult any one of a number of fine restaurant guides, from *Milwaukee Epicure*, which publishes menus, to the critiques in the newspapers and in *Milwaukee Magazine*.

Enjoy!

Fish Fries

Back when Catholics were forbidden to eat meat on Friday, restaurateurs, fraternal organizations and innkeepers began offering fish fries, which became a tradition embraced by Milwaukeeans, Catholic and nonCatholic alike. Here are some of our favorite Friday night fish fries that welcome families.

Country Garden Restaurant
911 West Layton Avenue (481-2420).
Reservations necessary. South.

Elm Grove Inn
13275 Watertown Plank Road (782-7090).
West.

Milwaukee Turners' Bar and Restaurant
1034 North Fourth Street (273-5590).
Smorgasbord served in the gymnasium. Downtown.

Port Road Inn
8615 North Port Washington Road (352-9442).
Reservations necessary. Northeast.

Range Line Inn
2635 West Mequon Road 112 N, Mequon (242-0530).
The word is out and it's good! The secret is in the batter. The lines can be long, so make reservations. Far north.

Selen's
3107 East Layton Avenue (744-7890).
South.

Serb Memorial Hall
5101 West Oklahoma Avenue (545-6030).
Served family-style. Southwest.

Tanner Paull Post — American Legion Bar and Restaurant
6922 West Orchard Street (476-0434).
There can be a bit of a wait, so make reservations. It's a basement with not much decor, but the kids liked it. South.

Downtown

Benihana of Tokyo
330 East Kilbourn Avenue (273-7899).

A lot of flash and dash! These aren't just tableside chefs, they're showmen. It's a bit expensive, but if you're celebrating, it's a good excuse to take the group.

Heinemann's
730 North Milwaukee Street (276-5622).
777 East Wisconsin Avenue (765-0200).
665 West Wisconsin Avenue (272-2520).

They all have high chairs and booster seats. No special menu for kids, but the food is simple, and we've never found it hard to please the whole group. The breads are delicious, and there's always the sundae with the crunch on the top that everybody wants to eat.

Milwaukee Turners Bar and Restaurant
1034 North Fourth Street (273-5590).
Good food; barnlike decor.

Palate Pleasers
135 West Wells Street (273-2273).

The restaurant is on the second floor and has huge windows. (The building itself is a delight.) Make a salad or order a sandwich. The clientele is mostly business people and there are no high chairs, but it's nice for older children.

Real Chili
419 East Wells Street (271-4042).
1625 West Wells Street (342-6955).
Chili any way you want it!

Rocky Rococo's Pan Style Pizza
330 East Wells Street (271-4777).

The Safe House
779 North Front Street (271-2007).

This is a good place for twitchy kids! They can explore all kinds of nooks and crannies; even going to the washroom is an adventure. The kids love it and it's a great place for a birthday party in off-hours (it's a bar), but be sure to arrange your party well in advance. The food literally drops from the ceiling in the back rooms.

Speisegarten, Grand Avenue Mall
West Wisconsin Avenue.
A potpourri of ethnic fast foods.

North

Boder's On The River
11919 North River Road 43W, Mequon (242-0335).

Homemade cherry muffins, corn fritters, and fresh fruit platters are specialties. A gracious meal in the country, though it's expensive. The grounds are lovely. Take time for a leisurely stroll.

Chi Chi's
7807 West Servite Plaza Court, across from Northridge (355-0900).

Mexican. No reservations taken.

Kurt Schultz's Delicatessen and Restaurant
8752 North Deerwood Road (354-1004).

Good sandwiches; eat there or carry out.

Port Road Inn
8615 North Port Washington Road (352-9442).

Delicious salad bar. A nice place to eat with children who can sit still.

Showbiz Pizza Place
7401 West Good Hope Road (358-2023).

Games and gorilla antics with pizza.

Tanglewood
6630 West Hampton Avenue (464-9700).

Go for the salad bar; a place to sit and dine. Lots of good food.

South

The Chancery Pub and Restaurant
4624 South 27th Street (282-3350).
Stained glass, lots of oak, and hamburgers in combinations you wouldn't believe.

Chi Chi's
5005 South 74th Street (423-0600).
Mexican. No reservations.

Chuck E Cheese Pizza Time Theatre
2701 South Chase Avenue (483-8655).
2990 South 108th Street (546-3600).
Pizza with mouse antics!

Conejito's
539 West Virginia Street (278-9106).
Good Mexican food. A diverse crowd that can be a bit boisterous. The older kids will be wide-eyed.

Dinner Bell
119 East Oklahoma Avenue (744-3004).
Family-style dinners.

Krokus Restaurant
2316 South Sixth Street (643-6383).
Authentic Polish dining.

Showbiz Pizza Place
4595 South 27th Street (281-1200).
See Showbiz — North.

Three Brothers Bar and Restaurant
2414 South St. Claire Street (481-7530).
An ethnic classic, family operated.

East

Beans and Barley
1901 East North Avenue (278-7878).
Vegetarian grocery and cafe; eat there or take it home.

Benjamin's Delicatessen
4156 North Oakland Avenue (332-7777).
Delicious Jewish deli. The corned beef sandwich is big enough to split to feed two small children, or just order a half sandwich.

Chili John's
2951 North Oakland Avenue (964-1122).
Chili and more chili!

Heinemann's
412 East Silver Spring Drive (964-6060).
See Heinemann's — Downtown.

La Casita
2014 North Farwell Avenue (227-1177).
Mexican fare; you can sit outside in the summer.

Rocky Rococo's Pan Style Pizza
5900 North Port Washington Road, in Bay Shore Mall (332-6070).
Pizza by the slice plus a good salad bar.

West Bank Cafe
732 East Burleigh Street (562-5555).
Seafood and chicken, and vegetarian fare. Light and airy decor.

West

The Black Kettle
8660 North 107th Street (354-8950).
A pretty place to eat and celebrate. The moderately priced menu includes sandwiches, and super homemade rolls that come with the salad.

The Chancery Pub & Restaurant
7613 West State Street (453-2300).
See the Chancery — South.

Chi Chi's
18365 West Bluemound Road (785-0666).
See Chi-Chi's — North.

Chuck E Cheese Pizza Time Theatre
2436 North 124th Street (782-5530).
See Chuck E Cheese Pizza Time Theatre — South.

Dick Manhardt's Inn
14000 West North Avenue (786-5440).
A local family eatery in Brookfield.

Heinemann's
317 North 76th Street (258-6800).
See Heinemann's — Downtown.

Houlihan's Old Place
95 Moorland Road (784-7373).
A bar that is family oriented. They have high chairs.

Omega Family Restaurant
5081 South 108th Street, Hales Corners (425-5177).
Homemade soups. Good food and a good value. Open 24 hours.

The Proud Popover
17700 West Capitol Drive, in Stonewood Village (781-1776).
Oodles of popovers, good soups and homemade potato chips.

Seigo's Japanese Steak House
18380 West Capitol Drive (781-2727).
Hibachi preparation tableside. They put on a good show and the food is delicious.

8
Escape From Milwaukee

By now, you've probably done everything in this book; so, spread your wings, gas up the car, and go. We have selected a few special places that are approximately 100 miles more or less from Milwaukee. If you feel more ambitious, call the Wisconsin Division of Tourism (toll-free 1-900 E-S-C-A-P-E-S) to request their superb booklet "Wisconsin: Auto Tour Escapes." We loved it!

Aztalan

Aztalan State Park
On Highway Q, three miles east of Lake Mills.
- Open May-October daily 10am-5pm.
- Admission, fee.

This is the site of an archaeological excavation uncovering an ancient Indian fort and village. The nearby museum contains Indian and pioneer objects. Park experts may be on hand to identify artifacts from private collections. Aztalan State Park is a good place to stop when you are traveling to New Glarus or Madison.

Baraboo

Circus World Museum
426 Water Street (608/356-8341).
- Open May–mid-September daily 9:30am-6pm.
- Admission, fee.

The main attraction of the day will be the circus performance under the big top. Stroll among the elaborate circus wagon collection, talk to the clowns, and listen to the calliope. This is one of our longer trips, but we've done it in one day. Take the Merrimac Ferry across the Wisconsin River in Merrimac. It runs 24 hours a day until December, or extreme cold. It's a ten-minute ride.

Chicago

For a change of pace, head South. Within 100 miles you'll find Chicago: 8,000,000 people, 29 miles of Lake Michigan shoreline, and skyline jewels. Three of the world's tallest buildings are there: the 110-story Sears Tower, the 100-story John Hancock Center and the 80-story Standard Oil Building. Go to the top of the John Hancock for an aerial view of the city. Chicago is designed in a simple grid pattern, with the "El" (elevated trains) circling the "Loop" (downtown business district). Most streets run north-south or east-west. State Street and Madison Street are the zero-zero point, with street numbers ascending in all directions at approximately 100 numbers to each block.

Touring in the downtown area is relatively simple because of the availability of buses and taxis. Museums, art galleries, theatres, shopping and entertainment are easily accessible from the Loop. Drive down or take the train. AMTRAK (414/933-3081) offers a 6:55am train to Chicago, with returns at 4:30pm or 7:15pm; times and fares are subject to change. If you go by train, start your Chicago trip by spending ten extra minutes touring Union Station. If you just follow the crowd off the train and up to the street, you'll have missed the best part of Union Station. See the first floor waiting room area. It's timeless and expansive. If you drive down, there is a municipal parking lot east of the Chicago Art Institute in Grant Park that is centrally located.

- Area Code for Chicago is 312.
- Chicago Information and Tourism Bureau (225-2323).
- Curtain Call Theatre Information Line (977-1730).
- F-I-N-E-A-R-T/ Art Gallery Information (346-3278).
- R.T.A./ Public Transportation Route Information (836-7000).
  Inquire about shuttle bus service between the museums.
- Traveler's Aid (435-4500, 686-7562).
- Visitor Information (225-5000).

Adler Planetarium
1300 South Lake Shore Drive (312/322-0300).
In the Soldier's Field area.

- Open daily 9:30am-4:30pm, Fridays 9:30am-9pm. Closed Thanksgiving and Christmas.
- Building admission, free; Sky Show, fee; over 65, free.
- Parking available.
- Handicapped accessibility.

The public sky shows are scheduled every hour beginning at 11am. Children under 6 are not admitted to the Sky Show. A special children's Sky Show for preschoolers and their families is presented Saturdays at 10am.

Art Institute of Chicago
215 South Michigan Avenue (312/443-3600, 443-3500 for recorded message on exhibitions and lectures).

- Open Monday, Tuesday, Wednesday and Friday 10:30am-4:30pm; Saturday 10am-5pm; Thursday 10:30am-8pm; Sunday and holidays noon-5pm; closed Christmas Day.
- Discretionary admission fee; Thursday, free; special exhibits, separate admission.
- Group tours may be arranged in advance.
- Look for parking lots as you go east of Michigan Avenue on Monroe Street.
- Picnic Room and cafeteria.
- Especially nice gift shop.
- Wheelchair entrance at the Columbus Drive entrance.

Chinatown
West Cermak Road at South Wentworth Street.

- Free parking at Cermak and Wentworth, courtesy of the Chinese Merchants' Association.

A treat for your senses — smell the spices, see the street signs in Chinese, taste Oriental specialties, and poke around in the varied shops. If your Chinese isn't fluent, you can always point and guess.

Field Museum of Natural History
South Lake Shore Drive at Roosevelt Road (312/922-9410).

- Open Saturday-Thursday 9am-6pm, Friday 9am-9pm.
- Admission, fee; Friday, free.
- Free parking.
- Food service.
- Handicapped accessibility.

You can't miss the dinosaur skeleton. On the lower level seek out the mummy collection and the touch-and-feel room. A trip to the Field Museum combines nicely with the Shedd Aquarium and the Adler Planetarium; these three attractions are located in the same area. You can walk from one to the other, and along the way you'll have a spectacular view of the Chicago skyline.

Lincoln Park Zoo
Off the Outer Drive at Fullerton; 2200 North Cannon Drive (312/294-4660).

- Open daily 9am-5pm; Great Ape House, Childrens' Zoo, and Farm-in-the-Zoo open 10am-5pm.
- Admission, free.
- Meter parking, 25¢ per hour.
- Snacks available.
- Handicapped accessibility.

Special activities on Sundays. Free outdoor summer concerts (312/935-6700). Also, special summer activities held daily for children.

Museum of Contemporary Art
237 East Ontario Street (312/280-2660).

- Open Tuesday-Saturday 10am-5pm, Sunday noon-5pm.
- Admission, fee; Tuesday, free.
- Handicapped accessibility.

The museum is located in an area with a variety of fine art galleries. Parking is difficult; public transportation is recommended.

Museum of Science and Industry
South Lake Shore Drive at East 57th Street (312/684-1414).

- Open daily 9:30am-5:30pm.
- Admission, free; some exhibits, separate fee.
- Parking available.
- Food service.
- Handicapped accessibility.

Push the buttons, communicate with computers, and participate in many exhibits. A favorite of children.

Polish Museum of America
984 North Milwaukee, Chicago 60622 (312/278-3210), just off the Kennedy Expressway at Augusta.

- Open daily 12 noon-5pm.
- Guided tours may be arranged in advance; contact the curator (312/384-3352).
- Admission, free.

Ravinia Music Festival
See "Music-Instrumental" in Chapter 5.

Shedd Aquarium
1200 South Lake Shore Drive (312/939-2426).

- Open daily 9am-5pm, Friday 9am-9pm.
- Admission, fee; Friday, free to all.
- Park at the Field Museum and walk through that tunnel under the Outer Drive.

Unless you've been scuba diving in exotic places, you'll see shapes and colors you can't imagine. This is the "world's largest indoor aquarium." Divers feed the fish in the 90,000-gallon coral reef at 11am and 2pm daily.

Spertus Museum of Judaica
618 South Michigan Avenue (312/922-9012).

- Open Monday-Thursday 10am-5pm, Friday 10am-3pm, Sunday 10am-4pm.
- Admission, fee; Friday, free to all.
- Group tours; call in advance.

Watertower Place
835 North Michigan Avenue

Stroll down Michigan Avenue and enjoy the elegant shops. Spend time in Watertown Place and savor the gracious stores and architecture. There is ample opportunity to snack or dine. It dwarfs the nearby original water tower which is the only structure to have survived the Great Chicago Fire.

Performing Arts in Chicago
The variety is endless; here are a few.
- ▶ Curtain Call/Theatre Information (312/977-1755).
- ▶ Hot Tix (Full-price advance, half-price same day)
  24 South State Street Mall, Monday-Saturday 10am-4pm.
- American Chamber Symphony
  20 North Wacker Drive (312/236-7347).
- Arie Crown Theatre
  McCormick Place On-The-Lake (312/791-6000).
- The Blackstone Theatre
  60 East Balboa Drive (312/977-1720).
- Candlelight Dinner Playhouse
  5620 South Harley Avenue, Summit (312/496-3000).
- Chicago City Ballet
  223 West Erie Street (312/943-1315).
- Chicago Symphony Orchestra (312/435-8111).
- Civic Theatre/Opera House
  20 North Wacker Drive (312/559-1212, 346-0270).
- DePaul/Goodman School of Drama
  2324 North Fremont (312/321-8455).
- Drury Lane Oak Brook/Martinique Restaurants
  1919 South Highland, Lombard (312/530-0202).
- Goodman Theatre
  200 South Columbus Drive (312/443-3800).
- Grant Park/Petrillo Music Shell
  Jackson Boulevard and Columbus Drive (312/294-2493). Free outdoor summer concerts.
- Lyric Opera of Chicago
  20 North Wacker Drive (Civic Opera House) (312/332-2244).
- Loyola University Theatre
  6525 North Sheridan Road (312/508-3847).
- Marriott's Lincolnshire Theatre
  West of I-94 at Lincolnshire (312/634-0200).
- Northwestern University Theatre
  1979 Sheridan Road, Evanston (312/492-7282).
- Ravinia Pavilion and Theatre
  Exit Edens Expressway east on Lake-Cook Road, Highland Park (312/782-9696).
- Second City
  1616 North Wells Street. Parental discretion advised. (312/337-3992).
- Shubert Theatre
  22 West Monroe Street. (312/977-1720).

Dodgeville

See Mineral Point, below.

Eagle

Old World Wisconsin (State Historical Society of Wisconsin)
Route 2, Box 18, Eagle 53119 (414/594-2116).
I-94 west to Oconomowoc; south on Highway 67; 1½ miles south of Eagle in Waukesha County; 35 miles from downtown Milwaukee.

- Open daily May 1-October 31; May, June, September and October 9am-4pm; July, August and all weekends 10am-5pm.
- Admission, fee.
- Call or write in advance for school or bus tour reservations.
- Ample free parking.
- Clausing Barn Restaurant/Cafeteria on premises; picnic facilities.
- Gift shop.
- Handicapped accessibility limited by gravel roads and distance.

The farms, homes, institutions and a village of early Wisconsin settlers are recreated in this outdoor ethnic museum. The structures were collected from all over Wisconsin and restored on the 576-acre site. Visitors can smell fermenting sauerkraut, watch a farmhand dig a garden, taste freshly-churned sweet butter and listen to the whistle of a huge steam engine at threshing time. Don't miss the schoolhouse, but be on your best behavior — the teacher is strict. The minimum route of two to five miles of gravel road and woodland trails will tire a toddler and some grandparents. For an additional $1.00 per person, shuttle trams run every half hour on the interior roads. Plan to spend a full day. Call ahead to find out what special weekend events are scheduled.

Elkhart Lake

This old resort town offers many dining opportunities at the end of your day's outing. Stop in at the Chamber of Commerce office located in the Train Depot/Museum for more information.

Road America
Several miles south of town, off Highway 67.
Before this internationally known race track was built, the cars used to race through the streets of the town. Now the big event is held mid-summer with competitors from just about everywhere.

Firemans Park
On Highway A.
Swim in a clear glacial lake or hike the Potawatomi Indian Trail, a five-mile circle of the lake.

Fond du Lac

Galloway House and Village
336 Old Pioneer Road 54935 (414/922-6390).

- Open Memorial Day-September Tuesday-Sunday 1-4 pm.
- Admission, fee.

This 30-room classic Midwest version of an Italianate villa was built in 1847 and restored in 1880. It is surrounded by a village of nineteenth-century shops. Wander through a general store, photography studio, church, and shops. Volunteers will guide your tour and answer questions.

Gurnee, Illinois

Great America
Just off I-94 at Gurnee (312/249-1776).

- Open May-September; hours may vary according to time of year.
- Admission, fee.

This large amusement park has been designed to appeal to many ages. Plan to arrive early and spend the day. No picnicking is allowed in the park. It's not a bad idea to phone ahead to see if your favorite ride is operating. Watch for promotional coupons to cut costs.

Greenbush

Old Wade House (State Historical Society of Wisconsin)
Route 23 and Center Street 53026 (414/526-3271).

- Open May-October 9am-5pm; last tour 4:30pm.
- Admission, fee; children under 5, free.

The Wade House Inn was built in 1851 to serve travelers on the busy Sheboygan-Fond du Lac plank road. Costumed interpreters participate in activities, chores, and entertainments of 125 years ago. Ride a horse-drawn carriage to the Jung Carriage Museum. You might also wish to drive the nearby Kettle Moraine Scenic Drive.

Horicon

Horicon Marsh
Highway 41 north, then west on Highway 33; the marsh is located between the cities of Horicon and Waupun.

The overwhelming sight of several hundred thousand noisy migrating Canada geese, honking, flapping, strutting, taking off, and landing, is a Wisconsin must in October. Take a camera and field glasses. For peak season viewing dates, directions, and hiking reservations, contact:

▶ Horicon National Wildlife Refuge
  Rt. 2, Mayville, Wisconsin 53050 (414/387-2658, 387-2664).
▶ Blue Heron Boat Tours
  Highway 33, Horicon (414/485-2942).

- Tours daily April-October 2pm.
- Admission, fee.

Kenosha

American Motors
5626 25th Avenue, Kenosha 53140 (414/658-7680).
- Tours Monday-Friday 9:45am and 1pm; closed June-September, holidays, and Christmas vacation. Call ahead for reservations.

Civil War Museum
Carthage College, Lentz Hall, Kenosha 53141 (414/551-8500).
- Open Monday-Friday 8am-4pm; Saturday 8am-noon.

Factory Outlet Center
Exit I-94 at Highway 50.
- 34 stores.

Kemper Pier
On the Lakefront.
- 161-foot fishing pier for the handicapped.

King Richard's Faire
Exit I-94 at Highway V (414/396-4385).
- Seasonal event, open July–mid-August.
- Admission, fee; under 5, free.

A return to the Renaissance: theatricals, music, dance, crafts, food, and drinks of the sixteenth century.

Kohler/Sheboygan

John Michael Kohler Art Museum
608 New York Avenue, Sheboygan 53081 (414/458-6144).
- Open daily year-round noon-5pm.

Check for scheduling of plays, musical events, and the annual outdoor art festival.

Kohler-Andrae State Park
I-43 at Highway KK, 7 miles south of Sheboygan.

Take a picnic and go to the beach (no lifeguards); dig your toes in the sandy dunes; visit the nature center and relax.

Kohler Company
Highland Drive, Kohler 53044 (414/457-4441 ext. 2243).
- Tours by reservation only, Monday-Thursday 9am; age 14 and older.

Manufacturers of fine plumbing fixtures and so much more. You'll love the showroom! Try the tubs out for size.

Kohler Village
(414/457-4441 ext. 2243).
- Tours April-October Tuesday-Thursday 1pm; November-March Tuesday 1pm. Reservations required well in advance.

One of the first planned communities in the United States, this is a company town. The renovated American Club is a showplace; ask about its history. Elegant dining — even the soda shop in the courtyard is a treat.

Sheboygan County Museum
3110 Erie Drive, Sheboygan (414/458-1103).
- Open April-October, Tuesday-Saturday 10am-5pm, Sunday 1-5pm.
- Admission, fee.

Waelderhaus
West Riverside Drive, Kohler 53044 (414/452-4079).
- Open year-round; closed holidays. Tours daily 2pm, 3pm, and 4pm; reservations required.

Reproduction of the Kohler family ancestral home in Austria.

Madison

The Capitol
(608/266-0382)
- Open year-round except major holidays; tours on the hour 9am-4pm except noon. Look for the dome!

Observation platform provides a panoramic view of the city; ask if it's open. Before you leave the capitol building, inquire if tours are being given that day at the Governor's Mansion.

- ►Special feature: G.A.R. Memorial Hall Museum (608/266-1680). Open year-round Monday-Friday 9am-4:30pm. Civil and Spanish-American War exhibits.

Capitol Square
- ►Capitol Carriage Horse and Buggy Rides
  Wisconsin Avenue (608/255-5845).
  - May, Saturday 1-6pm, Sunday 1-5pm; June-October, Wednesday-Friday 3-8pm, Saturday-Sunday 1-5pm, weather permitting.
  - Admission, fee.
- ►Farmer's Market
  - May-October Saturday mornings.

Governor's Mansion
99 Cambridge Road.
- For tour information call the Capitol (608/266-0382).

For a seasonal treat, try the candlelight Christmas tours.

Olbrich Botanical Gardens
3330 Atwood Avenue (608/266-4731).
- Open May-September 9am-dusk.
- Garden for the visually handicapped.

A romantic place to stroll.

State Historical Society
816 State Street (608/262-9567).
- Open year-round Monday-Thursday 9am-9pm, Friday-Saturday 9am-5pm, Sunday noon-5pm; closed holidays and UW vacations.
- Gift shop.

University Book Store
711 State Street at Lake Street
- Open Monday-Saturday 9am-5pm. Browsing for bibliophiles.

University of Wisconsin-Madison
▶ Arboretum-McKay Center, Longenecker Horticultural Gardens (608/263-7888).
- Open year-round Monday-Friday 7am-4pm, Saturday-Sunday 12:30-4pm. Tours May-September, Sunday; call for reservations.

▶ Babcock Hall
At Babcock and Linden drives.
- Open weekdays. Treat yourself to some of the best ice cream and yogurt in the Midwest.

▶ Camp Randall Stadium
Athletic ticket office is at Monroe Street entrance (608/262-1440).
- Go to a game. It's more than football!

▶ Elvehjem Museum of Art
800 University Avenue (608/263-2246).
- Open year-round Monday-Saturday 9am-4:45pm, Sunday 11am-4:45pm; closed holidays.

▶ Walking Tour
Memorial Union (at Langdon and Park streets) second floor information desk. Call for an appointment (608/262-2511).

Vilas Park Zoo
702 South Randall Avenue (608/266-4732).
- Open in summer, 9:30am-8pm; in winter, 9:30am-5pm.

Mineral Point/Dodgeville

While in Mineral Point, ask where you can taste and buy Julie Hook's award-winning Colby cheese.

Pendarvis (State Historical Society of Wisconsin)
114 Shake Rag Street, Mineral Point 53565 (608/987-2122).
- Open daily May-October, 10am-5pm.
- Admission, fee.

A century-and-a-half ago, Pendarvis was a rough and tough lead-mining region. Visit the restored homes and pubs of Cornish miners. You can stop to sample the traditional lead miner's meal, a cornish pasty, at the Mineral Point Bakery.

The Looms
Shake Rag Street, Mineral Point 53565
- Open daily May-October 15, 9am-5pm.
- Admission, fee.

Once an old brewery, it is now a museum of spinning and weaving equipment. Weavers demonstrate their craft.

Governor Dodge State Park
Highway 23, Dodgeville.

This huge state park (5,000 acres) has special features. Bring your hiking boots and climb the cliffs. Look for fossils. Enjoy the spectacular panoramic views. The camping sites are spectacular; reserve well in advance. (See "camping" in Chapter 3.)

New Glarus

Taste the delicacies at the Swiss restaurants and bakery.

Swiss Historical Village
612 Seventh Avenue (608/527-2317).
- Open daily May-October 9am-5pm.
- Admission, fee.

Wander through a replica of a pioneer village settled by the Swiss in 1845.

North Lake

Kettle Moraine Scenic Steam Train
Exit I-94, north on Highway 83. (414/782-8074, 966-2866)
- Open Sundays June 5-October 16, plus July 4 and Labor Day; departures 1pm, 2:30pm, and 4pm, rain or shine.
- Admission, fee; group rates available.
- Free parking.
- Picnic area.
- Handicapped accessibility.

Enjoy a 75-minute nostalgic ride on an antique trian pulled by a steam engine. Your outing might include a visit to nearby Holy Hill and a stop at Honey Acres for a sweet treat. (see Chapter 2).

Oshkosh

EAA Aviation Center
3000 Poberezny Road (414/426-4800).
- Open year-round Monday-Saturday 8:30am-5pm, Sunday 11am-5pm; closed holidays.
- Admission, fee.

The Experimental Aircraft Association encourages the flying and building of aircraft as well as the preservation of classic airplanes. People come from all over for the summer EAA Fly-In and Convention. Neat aircraft on display!

Oshkosh B'Gosh, Inc.
1331 Algoma Boulevard (414/231-8800).
- Open year-round Tuesday-Thursday 10:30am and 2:30pm, one day's notice required.
- Admission, free.
- Off-street parking.
- Handicapped accessibility.

Watch them make those overalls, b'gosh!

Paine Art Center and Arboretum
1410 Algoma Boulevard (414/235-4530).
- Open year-round Tuesday-Sunday 10am-4:30pm, Sunday 1-4:30pm; closed most holidays.
- Guided tours must be arranged two weeks in advance.
- Admission, $1.00 donation requested.

Can you imagine an English Tudor manor house that is 31,000 square feet and is surrounded by a 15-acre arboretum? This lavish estate is now a museum for you to tour. It is on the National Register of Historic Places. A rich portrait of a bygone era!

Racine

If you visit in the summer, you might want to stop at Quarry Lake Park (see Chapter 4). On Lake Michigan, at Kewaunee Street, you'll find North Beach, a four-star beach a stone's throw from the Racine Zoo.

Johnson Wax/Golden Rondelle Theatre
14th and Franklin Streets, Racine 53403 (414/631-2154).
- Advance registration for tours is necessary, call or write. Three tours offered per day Monday-Friday, closed holidays; age 14 and older.
- Admission, free.
- Handicapped accessibility.

Take an architectural tour of the Frank Lloyd Wright-designed Administration Building. Arrange to see a film in the Golden Rondelle Theatre, which was designed for the 1964-65 World's Fair.

Sheboygan

See Kohler, this chapter.

Spring Green

American Players Theatre
Highway C and Golf Course Road (608/588-2361, 588-7401).
- For performance schedule, food, lodging and tourist attractions, write American Players Theatre, Route 3, Spring Green, Wisconsin 53588.

The focus is on Shakespeare in this outdoor theatre. The setting in the rolling, wooded hills is beautiful, but can be a bit buggy. Take insect repellent. You don't have to be a Shakespeare buff to enjoy these plays.

Frank Lloyd Wright Buildings
c/o Taliesin, Spring Green 53588 (608/588-2511).
- Tour late June-Labor Day 10am-4pm; Taliesin is not on the tour.
- Admission, fee.

House on the Rock
Highway 23, Spring Green (608/935-3639).
• Open April–mid-November 8am-2 hours before dusk.
• Admission, fee.

Tower Hill State Park
Highway C near Spring Green.
See the tower used for making lead bullets during Civil War days.

Watertown
Octagon House
919 Charles Street (414/261-2796).
• Open Friday, Saturday and Sunday, 10am-5pm.
• Admission, fee; under age 6, free.

Fifty-seven rooms (including closets and halls) center around an open spiral stairway with a cherrywood banister. This imposing house is the largest pre-Civil War house in Wisconsin. Also on the grounds is America's first kindergarten building (1856).

Wisconsin Dells
I-90/94 exit #89 or #87 east to Highway 12.
This is as far as we would recommend for a one-day trip (it's about 160 miles), but we've done it. There is a variety of activities; all charge a fee. Pick and choose according to the ages in your family. Here are a few of our favorites:

Storybook Gardens
Preschoolers like its gentle touches. Help Bo-Peep find her sheep. Open 10am-6:30pm.

Fort Dells
School-aged kids love it. Be on the lookout for stagecoach robbers and bad hombres.

Water Ski Shows
• Handicapped accessibility.

Tommy Bartlett, local promoter, presents several shows. Our favorite is the "Ski, Sky, and Stage Show." Our kids sat quietly (a miracle!) for 90 minutes, entranced by the daredevils.

Stand Rock Indian Ceremonial
This program has been around for generations. For us, it evokes fond memories of traditional dances, colorful costumes, and Indian lore. Go by car or boat; performances begin at 8:45pm.

River Tours
Two good ways to see the magnificent rock formations and water canyons along the Wisconsin River are the "Ducks" (amphibious vehicles), and the tour boats. We recommend the longer boat tours, which allow you to disembark at several points and climb around; it's worth the extra cost.

Noah's Ark
If you're in the Dells area or even traveling I-94 on a hot day, here's a great way to cool off. Stop and try the giant water slide. The trip down swirls and twirls through tunnels and corkscrews. For the timid, there is a less awesome slide. The well-planned dressing facilities make the logistics of a pit stop easy. Open 9am-midnight.

9
Index

A

Acacia Theatre Company, 102
Adler Planetarium (Chicago), 132, 133
Admirals, Milwaukee, 73
Afro Fest, 92
Airport, General Mitchell Field, 56
Airport Firehouse, 56
Allen Edmonds Shoe Bank Bootery, 116
Allis Art Museum, Charles, 4
Alpine Valley Music Theater, 88, 96
Al's Run, 83
Alverno College, 88
Ambrosia Chocolate Factory Outlet Store, 112
American Club, 138
American Geographical Society Collection (UW-M), 107
American Motors (Kenosha), 138
American Players Theatre (Spring Green), 142
American Saddle Horse Show, 109
American Science Center, 120
Amity/Enger-Kress Outlet Store, 119
AMTRAK, 58, 132
AMTRAK - tours, 58
amusement park (Great America), 137
animal shelter, Humane Society, 57
Annunciation Greek Orthodox Church, 21, 90
apple picking, 22
Aquarium, Shedd (Chicago), 133, 134
Arabian Horse Show, Wisconsin, 109
Arboretum (Madison), 140
archeological excavation, 131
archery, 65, 75
Archi-Tours, 25, 27
Arenz Cutlery, 120
Arlington Park (Chicago), 25
Art Galleries (UW-M), 107
Art History Gallery (UW-M), 107
Art Institute (Chicago), 133
Artist Series at the Pabst, 96
Art Museum, Milwaukee, 2, 12, 105, 106
Art Museum, Paine (Oshkosh), 142
Art Museum (UW-M), 107
art supplies, 120
Ashippun, 56, 63
Asian Mart, 112
Astronomical Society Observatory, 54
auctions, 118
Audubon Center, 67
auto tours, 27
Auto Tour Escapes, Wisconsin, 131
Aztalan State Park (Aztalan), 131

B

Babcock Hall (Madison), 140
Badgerland Striders, 83
Bagel Nosh Delicatessen, 112
Balkan Trading Company, 112
Ballet Company, Milwaukee, 20, 104
Ballfour Cards, 121
band concerts, 106
Baraboo, 131
Barthel Fruit Farm, 115
Bartlett Water Ski Shows (Wisconsin Dells), 143
Bartz Displays Inc., 121
baseball, 72, 75
Basilica, St. Josaphat's, 22
basketball, 72
Bastille Day, 90
Bauer Dance Company, 104
Bayshore shopping center, 120
beaches, 85, 86
Beans and Barley, 112, 128
Bel Canto Chorus, 99
Benihana of Tokyo, 125
Benjamin's Delicatessen, 128
Best, Jacob, 15
Betty's Bead Bank, 121
bicycle racing, 73
bike trails, 75-79
biking, 75
bird watching, 63, 67-68, 137
Birkebeiner, 84
Bits of Britain, 112
Black Kettle Restaurant, 129
Blatz, Valentine, 15
Blizzard Ski Club, 85
Blue Heron Boat Tours (Horicon), 137
boating, 80
boat launching, 80, 84
boat trips, 26, 137, 144
Bodamer Log Cabin Museum, 3
Boder's on the River, 126
Boelter, F.W., Restaurant Supplies, 122
Boerner Botanical Gardens, 63-64
Bonne Bell Run, 83
book sales, used, 18
Botanical Gardens (The Domes), 66
Botanical Gardens (Madison), 139
bowling, 80
bowling, lawn, 80
boxing, 73
box office telephone numbers, 88
Boy Scout Museum, 6
Bradley Sculpture Garden Tour, 3
Brady Street, 46, 49-50

Branovan Shoe Company, 116
Brasslight, 20
Bravo Milwaukee, 25
Brewers, Milwaukee, 72
brewery tours, 54
Broadway Auction Gallery, 118
Brookfield Players, 101
Brookfield Square, 119
Brooks Stevens Automotive Museum, 3
Brown Bach It, 106
Brown Bag Film Series, 106
Brownberry Ovens, 116
Brown Deer Park, 81
Bucks, Milwaukee, 72
Burlington Coat Factory Warehouse, 117
bus routes (Chicago), 132
bus routes (Milwaukee), 25
bus tours, 25-28

C

Caesar's Park, 47
camping, 69, 80, 141
Camp Randall Stadium (Madison), 140
Canoe Association, Wisconsin, 80
Capitol, Wisconsin State (Madison), 139
Capitol Carriage Horse and Buggy Rides, 139
Capitol Court shopping center, 120
Capitol Square (Madison), 139
Cardinal Stritch College, 88, 107
Carroll College, 88, 99
cars - see Brooks Stevens Automotive Museum, 3
Carters, 116
Carthage College (Kenosha), 138
car wash, 109
Catholic Symphony Orchestra, Milwaukee, 96
Cave of the Mounds, 80
caving, 80
Cedarburg, 14
Cedar Creek Settlement, 14, 118
Cedar Lake Campus House of Friendship, 4
Chagall, Marc, 6
Chamber Orchestra, Milwaukee, 96
Chamber Singers, 96
Chancery Pub and Restaurant, 127, 129
Chapel, St. Joan of Arc, 22
Charles Allis Art Museum, 4
Chess Club, Milwaukee, 92, 110
Chicago, 25-26, 58, 132-35
Chicago:
    Adler Planetarium, 132, 133

AMTRAK, 132
Art Institute, 133
Chinatown, 133
City Ballet, 135
Curtain Call Theatre Information, 132
Field Museum of Natural History, 133
F-I-N-E-A-R-T Art Gallery Information, 132
Hancock Center, John, 132
Information and Tourism Bureau, 132
Lincoln Park Zoo, 133
Museum of Contemporary Art, 134
Museum of Science and Industry, 134
Performing Arts, 134
Ravinia Music Festival, 134
R.T.A./Public Transportation Route Information, 132
Sears Tower, 132
Shedd Aquarium, 133
Spertus Museum of Judaica, 134
Symphony Orchestra, 96, 98
Traveler's Aid, 132
Union Station, 132
Visitor Information, 132
Watertower Place, 134
Chi Chi's, 126-27, 129
Children's Chorus, 99
Children's Hospital Tour, 57
Children's Theatre, 100
Children's Zoo, 70, 133
Chili John's, 128
Chinatown (Chicago), 133
Chip n' Pys, 20
Chocolate House, 116
Chocolate Swan Ltd., 112
Christian Union Baptist Church, 43
Christmas, 94-95
Christmas Carol, A, 17, 95
Christmas Parade, Downtown, 94
Chuck E Cheese Pizza Time Theatre, 127, 129
church bazaars, 89
circus parade, 91
Circus World Museum (Baraboo), 91, 131
City Hall, Milwaukee, 14
City of Festivals Parade, 89
Civic Music Association, 96
Civil War, 6, 138
Civil War Museum (Kenosha), 138
Clausing Barn Restaurant (Eagle), 136
Clavis Theatre Company, 102
Clothes Rack, 119
Club 41, 41
Club Garibaldi, 109
Coffee Trader, 112

Colby cheese, Julie Hook's, 140
College for Kids (UW-M), 107
Colnik, Cyril, 4, 7, 10, 12
Colnik Museum, 4
Community Theater, 101
Concordia College, 88
Conejito's, 127
Congregation Emanu-El B'ne Jeshurun, 21
Conservatory of Music, Wisconsin, 99
Convent of the School Sisters of Notre Dame, 32
Conway, John, 16
Country Garden Restaurant, 124
County Courthouse and Safety Building, Milwaukee, 55
County Parks at a Glance chart, 65
County Sports Office, 75
Court Street Theater, 102
Craft Centre (UW-M), 107
Cream City Cycle Club, 75
cross country ski trails, 65, 67, 68, 70, 84
Cudahy Nature Preserve, 66
curling, 81
Curling Clubs (Milwaukee, Waukesha, Wauwatosa), 81
Curtain Call/Theatre Information Line (Chicago), 132
Curtin House, Jeremiah, 7
custard, 109

D

dairy farm tours, 56
Damon House, Lowell, 8
dance, 104
Dancecircus, 104
Delco Electronics, 55
Dells, Wisconsin, 143
Department of City Development, Milwaukee, 21
Department of Natural Resources, Wisconsin, 69, 81, 82
Dick Dahlman's Antiques and Reproductions, 121
Dick Manhardt's Inn, 129
Dick Shore Dinner Theatre, 102
Dinner Bell, 127
dinner theater, 102
Dinosaur Dash, 83
dinosaurs, 5, 9
disc golf, 81
Discover Milwaukee: Auto Tours, 27
DiSuvero sculpture, 14
DNR, 69, 81, 82

Dodgeville, 136, 140, 141
dog show, 108
Domes, The, 66
Dousman-Dunkle-Behling House, 5
Downer Avenue, 118
Downtown Christmas Parade, 94
Dressing Down, 116
ducks, 63, 144

E

EAA Aviation Center (Oshkosh), 141
Eagle, 136
Eagles Club, 73
Easter Seal Society: programs, 64; Shop, 121
East Library, 47
East Side Walking Tour, 46-53
Edgewood Agency, 100
Elderhostel, 107
Elkhart Lake, 86, 136
Elmbrook Historical Society, 5
Elm Grove Inn, 124
Elvehjem Museum of Art (Madison), 140
Emanu-El B'ne Jeshurun, Congregation, 21
Embroiderers Guild of America, 100
Emerald Isle Boat Line, 26
Empire Fish, 112
equestrian events, 109
Eschweiler, Alexander, 4
ethnic festivals, 88
European Village, 9
Everitt Knitting Mills, 116
exercise courses, 65
Exotic Plant Sale, 66
Experimental Aircraft Association, 141
Explorers Shop (West Bend), 119

F

Factory Outlet Center (Kenosha), 117, 138
Factory Outlet Cookware (West Bend), 119
factory outlets, 116, 117, 119
farmer's markets: 36, 115; Madison, 139; West Allis, 114
feed the ducks, 63
Fein's Restaurant Supply, 122
ferryboat (Merrimac), 131
Festa Italiana, 91
Fiberesin, 116
Field Museum of Natural History (Chicago), 133
Fiesta Mexicana, 93
figure skating clubs, 83
films (UW-M), 105

Film Series, Art Museum, 3, 105
F-I-N-E-A-R-T/Art Gallery Information (Chicago), 132
Fine Arts Galleries (UW-M), 107
Fine Arts Quartet (UW-M), 98
Finney Library, 38
Firemans Park (Elkhart Lake), 86, 136
Fire Prevention Week, 55
Fireside Playhouse (Fort Atkinson), 88, 102
fire stations, 55, 59
First Wisconsin Center, 15
fish fries, 124
fishing, 81
Florentine Opera, 99
Fly-In and Convention, EAA, 141
folk dancing, 104, 109
Folk Fair, 94
Fond du Lac County, 137
Foods of All Nations, 112
football, 73
Forest Home Avenue, 29
Forest Home Cemetery, 15
Forest Home Library, 29
Fort Dells (Wisconsin Dells), 143
fossils, 5
Fox and Hounds Restaurant, 22
Friends Mime Theatre, 102
frisbee golf, 81
frozen custard, 109

G

Gallery Cinema, 105
Galloway House and Village (Fond du Lac), 137
G.A.R. Memorial Hall Museum (Madison), 139
geese, 137
genealogical research, 5, 7, 12, 26
Genealogical Research Library, 7
General Mitchell Field, 56
geology, 5
George Watts, 110, 121
George Watts Tea Room, 110, 121
German Fest, 93
Germantown Historical Museum, 5
Gibbsville Cheese Factory (Sheboygan Falls), 112
Gilles Frozen Custard, 109
Gimbels/M.A.C.C. Fund Run, 83
Glorioso's Market, 113
Golda Meir Library, 107
Golden Gloves Amateur Boxing, 73
Goldmann's Department Store, 121

golf, 64, 65, 81
gospel music, 92
Governor Dodge State Park (Dodgeville), 69, 141
Governor's Mansion (Madison), 139
Grain Exchange, 16
Grand Avenue Mall, 16, 120
Grand Avenue Mall Speisegarten, 16
Gray Line Tours, 25
Great America (Gurnee, Illinois), 137
Great American Children's Theatre, 100
Great Ape House, 133
Great Circus Parade, 91
Greater Milwaukee Funline, 88
Great Lakes Futons, 121
Greek festivals, 21, 90
Green Bay Packers, 73
Greenbush, 137
Greendale, 4
Greendale Suburban Players, 101
Greene Memorial Museum, 5
Greenfield, 3
Greenfield Historical Society, 3
Green Meadows Farm, 56, 115
Gromme, Owen, 58
Gurnee, Illinois, 137
gymnastics, 81, 107

H

Haggerty Museum of Art, 6
Hales Corners, 63
Hancock Center, John (Chicago), 132
handicapped centers, 64
handicapped citizens programs, 64
Handweavers Show, Wisconsin, 4
Hansberry-Sands Theatre, 102
Harrington Beach State Park, 85
Hart Park, 81, 82
Harvey, Corrine A. Perrine, 20
Hawthorne Glen Nature Preserve, 66, 82
Heg Museum, 6
Heinemann's, 125, 128, 129
Herb Society of America Annual Plant Sale, 113
Heritage Museum, 6
hiking/walking, 81, 140
Historical Center, Milwaukee County, 7
Historical Society, State, 136, 137, 139, 140
Hoan Bridge Run, 83
hockey, 73
Holiday Folk Fair, 94
Holler Park, 64
Holy Hill, 141

Holy Hill Carmelite Monastery, 22, 56
Holy Rosary Catholic Church, 46, 51
Home Seekers Auto Tour, 27
Honey Acres, 22, 56, 113, 141
Hong Fat Company, 113
Horicon, 137
Horicon Marsh, 137
Horicon National Wildlife Refuge, 137
horseback riding, 82
horses, 109
hospital tours, 57
Hot Tix (Chicago), 135
Houlihan's Old Place, 129
House of Friendship, 4
House on the Rock (Spring Green), 143
Humane Society Animal Shelter, 57
Hunholz, Henry, 41, 42
hunting, 82

I

ice skating, 82
Indian burial mound, 17
Indian Ceremonial, 143
Indian groceries and spices, 113
Indian Mart Inc., 113
indoor ice chalet, 82
inland lakes, 86
Inner City Travel Company, 25
instrumental music, 96
International Institute, 94, 104
Irish Fest, 93
Iroquois Boat Tour, 26

J

Jacobus Park Handicapped Nature Trail, 82
Jalapeno Pepper Eating Contest, 93
Jazz Ensemble (UW-M), 98
Jazzy Lunches, 106
Jefferson Street, 118
Jeremiah Curtin House, 7
Jewish Community Center, 81, 91, 98, 103
Jewish Jubilee, 91
Jewish music, 98
jogging, 83
John Michael Kohler Art Museum (Sheboygan), 138
Johnson Wax/Golden Rondelle Theatre (Racine), 26, 142
J.U.M.P. Dance Theater, 104
Juneautown Opera, 99
Juneteenth Day, 89
Jung Carriage Museum (Greenbush), 137
Junior House factory outlet store, 116

K

Kahn's Clothing, 117
Kalvelage Schloss, 7
Karl Zeidler Park, 106
Kemper Pier (Kenosha), 138
Kenosha, 86, 138
Kenosha Factory Outlet Center, 138
Kettle Moraine Scenic Steam Train (North Lake), 56, 141
Kettle Moraine State Park, 80, 82, 137
Kid's Fest, 94
Kilbourntown House, 8
Kinder Cinema (UW-M), 105
Kinderkonzerts, 97
King Richard's Faire (Kenosha), 138
kite flying, 83
Kite Society of Milwaukee, 83
Kitt's Frozen Custard, 109
Kivitt, Ted, 104
Knit Pikker factory outlet store, 116
Kohler, 138
Kohler-Andrae State Park (Sheboygan), 80, 85, 138
Kohler Art Museum (Sheboygan), 138
Kohler Company, 138
Kohler Village, 138
Kolpacki, Bernard, 30, 31, 32, 49
Kopp's Frozen Custard, 109
Kosciuszko Junior High School, 33
Kosciuszko Park, 33
Kosciuszko, Thaddeus, 33
Ko Thi Dance, 104
Krokus Restaurant, 127
Kuppenheimer factory outlet store, 116
Kurt Schultz's Delicatessen and Restaurant, 126

L

Laacke and Joys, 121
La Casita, 128
Lakefront Festival of the Arts, 2, 89
Lake Mills, 131
Lake Park, 17
La Kermisse de la Bastille, 90
Lannon Quarry, 86
Larry's Brown Deer Market, 113
lawn bowling, 80
Leon's Frozen Custard, 109
Liberace Playhouse, 20
Library, Milwaukee Public, 18, 19, 69
Library Council of Metropolitan Milwaukee, 29
library hours, 18, 19

licenses, fishing, 81
Lighthouse, Northpoint, 17
Lincoln Center for the Arts, 88, 102, 103, 104
Lincoln Memorial Bridge, 106
Lincoln Park Zoo (Chicago), 133
Linden Room, 110
Lisbon Avenue, 39
Lite Beer Lake Front Marathon, 83
little league, 75
local theater companies, 101, 102, 103
Loehmann's, 117
Looms, The (Mineral Point), 140
Lowell Damon House, 8
lunchtime entertainment, 106

M

Mackie Building, 16
Madison, 131, 139
  Arboretum, 140
  Babcock Hall, 140
  Camp Randall Stadium, 140
  Capitol Carriage Horse and Buggy Rides, 139
  Capitol Square, 139
  Elvehjem Museum of Art, 140
  Farmers Market, 139
  G.A.R. Memorial Museum, 139
  Governor's Mansion, 139
  McKay Center, 140
  Olbrich Botanical Gardens, 139
  State Capitol, 139
  State Historical Society, 139
  University Book Store, 140
  University of Wisconsin, 140
  Vilas Park Zoo, 140
  Walking Tour, 140
magic show, 90
Manhardt's Inn — Dick, 129
Map Service, Milwaukee, 121
Market Place, The, 118
Marquette Place, Pere, 7
Marquette University, 6, 22, 72, 84, 88
Marquette University Warriors, 72
Marshall and Ilsley Bank tour, 58
Matthews Brothers, 7, 10, 12
Mauthe Lake, 86
Mayfair Mall Ice Chalet, 82
Mayfair Mall shopping center, 120
Mayville, 137
MECCA, 88, 94
MELCO clothing, 119
Melody Top Tent Theatre, 88, 100

Memorial Union (UW-Madison), 140
Menomonee Falls, 10
Menomonie Park Lannon Quarry (Lannon), 86
Men's Rugby Club, Milwaukee, 83
Mequon, 3
Merrimac ferry, 131
Messmer, Henry, 32
Metropolitan Ski Council, 85
Mila's K and K Bake Shop, 113
Miller Brewery, 44, 54
Miller-Davidson House, 10
Miller Highlife Summer Concerts, 96
Milwaukee:
  Admirals, 73
  Art Museum, Milwaukee, 2, 12, 105, 106
  Auction Gallery, 118
  Ballet Company, 20, 104
  Brewers, 72
  Bucks, 72
  Catholic Symphony Orchestra, 96
  Chamber Orchestra, 96
  Chess Club, 110
  Choristers, 99
  City Hall, 14
  Community Sailing Center, 84, 86
  County Astronomical Society Observatory, 54
  County Courthouse and Safety Building, 55
  County Department of Parks, Recreation and Culture, 11, 64
  County Extension Service, 68
  County Historical Center, 7
  County Stadium ticket office, 72, 73
  County Transit System Sightseeing Tours, 25
  County Zoo, 70, 84, 97
  Epicure,, 124
  fire stations, 55
  Hiking Club, 82
  Historical Center, County, 7
  Journal Public Service Desk, 96, 97
  Journal/Sentinel tour, 58
  Kickers, 85
  Map Service, 121
  Men's Rugby Club, 83
  Musical Arts Center, 7
  Opera, 99
  Paramedics tours, 59
  Players, 101
  Police Academy tours, 59
  Police Department tours, 59
  Polo Club, 73

Post Office tours, 61
Public Library, 18, 19, 69, 100
Public Museum, 9, 83, 105, 106
Public Museum Film Series, 105
Railroad Station tours, 58
Reflections, 25
Repertory Theatre, 17, 95, 102, 103
Rowing Club, 80
Sentinel Cycling Classic, 72
Sports Collector Store, 121
String Players Orchestra, 96
Symphony Orchestra, 90, 95, 97
Turners Bar and Restaurant, 124, 125
Turners School of Gymnastics, 81
Wave, 74
Wheelmen, 75
Women's Rugby Club, 83
Yacht Club, 84
Mineral Point, 140
Mitchell, Alexander, 16
Mitchell Field, 56
Mitchell Manufacturing, 119
Mitchell Park Horticultural Conservatory, 66
Mitchell Street, 35, 36
Mitchell Street Green Market, 36, 113
Modjeska Theatre, 36
Monastery, Holy Hill Carmelite, 22
Mount Mary College, 88
Mrs. Karl's Bakery, 117
Mukwonago Park, 86
Mukwonago Village Players, 101
Museum, Milwaukee County Public, 9, 83, 105, 106
Museum of Contemporary Art (Chicago), 134
Museum of Science and Industry (Chicago), 134
Music, 96-99
Music for Youth, 97
Music Under the Stars, 97
Muskego Town Hall Museum, 9
My Heart's at the Zoo, 70

N

Napoleon's, 121
National Register of Historic Places, 5, 10, 20
National Speleological Society, 80
nature preserves, 66
nature trails, 66
New Berlin, 13
New Berlin Auction and Sales Barn, 118
Newberry Brass Quintet, 97
New Glarus, 131, 141

newspaper tour, 58
New Year's Day, 110
Niemann's Homemade Chocolate Shop, 113
Noah's Ark water slide (Wisconsin Dells), 143
Nordic Ski Club of Milwaukee, 84
North Avenue, 44, 46, 47
North Lake, 141
Northpoint Historical Society tours, 28
Northpoint Lighthouse, 17
Northpoint Watertower, 17
Northridge shopping center, 120
North Shore Paramedics tours, 59
Nutcracker, The, 104

O

Oak Creek Community Theatre, 101
Oak Creek Historical Society Museum, 10
Oak Creek Power Plant tours, 61
Octagon House (Watertown), 143
Odds 'n' Ends shop, 119
Oktoberfest, 93
Olbrich Botanical Gardens (Madison), 139
Old Falls Village Museum, 10
Old Heidelberg Park, 93
Old Smokey, 17
Old Soldier's Home District, 20
Old Third Ward, 17, 46, 91
Old Wade House (Greenbush), 137
Old World Third Street, 95, 118
Old World Wisconsin (Eagle), 136
Olsen Planetarium, 108
Olympia Foods, 113
Olympic Polo Club, 73
Omega Family Restaurant, 129
On the Scene with Eleanor Woods and Associates, 26
opera, 99
Oriental Landmark Theatre, 46, 52, 105
Oriental Supreme Co., Inc., 113
Orlandini Studio, Ltd. tour, 58
Oshkosh, 141
Oshkosh B'Gosh, Inc., 141
Oster Company, 117
Our Lady of Pompeii Church, 46, 91
Outpost Natural Foods Co-op, 113
Ozaukee County Pioneer Village, 11

P

Pabst, Artist Series at the, 96
Pabst, Frederick, 10, 15, 17
Pabst Brewery, 54

Pabst Brewing Company, 94
Pabst Mansion, 10, 25
Pabst Theatre, 7, 17, 88
Packer Ticket Office, 23
PAC Programming for Young People, 100
Paine Art Center and Arboretum (Oshkosh), 142
Palate Pleasers, 125
Palette Shop, 120
parades, 89, 91, 94
Paradox Studio Theatre, 103
Paramedics tours, 59
Park-A-Beiner, 84
Park-It-Market, 117
Park People, 11, 64
Park Programs, 64
parks, 11, 33, 38-39, 63-66, 69-70, 75, 80-85
Parks at a Glance chart, 65
Parkside Lutheran Church, 38
Parkway Stables, 82
participation sports, 75
Peck Pavilion, 88, 106
Pendarvis (Mineral Point), 140
Penney, J.C., 117
Pepperidge Farm Thrift Shop, 117
Pere Marquette Park, 7
Performing Arts (Chicago), 134
Performing Arts Center (PAC), 88, 97, 98, 100, 103, 104, 106
Perhift Yiddish Theatre, 93
Peter Sciortino Bakery, 114
Pfister Hotel, 18
pick-your-own produce, 115
picnic areas, 65, 70
picnic permits, 64
Pig 'n' Whistle, 109
Pioneer Village of Ozaukee County, 11
Planetarium, Adler (Chicago), 132, 133
Planetarium, Olsen, 108
Plankinton Arcade, 16
poetry readings, 110
Point Loomis shopping center, 120
Polar Bear Swim, 110
Police Academy tours, 59
Police Department tours, 59
Polish Fest, 93
Polish flat, 29, 31, 46, 47, 49
Polish Museum of America (Chicago), 134
polo, 73
Polo Club, Milwaukee, 73
Port Road Inn, 124
Post Office tours, 61
Potawatomi Indian Trail, 136
Preoperation hospital tours, 57

Proud Popover restaurant, 129
Public Museum, Milwaukee County, 9, 83, 105, 106
Pulaski Street, 49

Q

Quarry Lake Park (Racine), 86, 142
Quarter Horse Show, Wisconsin, 109

R

Racine, 142
Racine, Tour About Inc., 26
Racine Zoo, 142
railroad station tours, 58
Rainbow Summer at the PAC, 98, 106
Range Line Inn, 124
Ravinia Music Festival (Highland Park, Illinois), 98, 134
Ravinia Theatre, 98
Real Chili, 125
Reel Art, Art Musem, 2, 105
Renaissance Book Shop, 122
Repertory Theatre, Milwaukee, 17, 95, 102, 103
restaurant supplies, 122
Richardson Romanesque, 13, 18
Riveredge Nature Center, 67, 82
Riverside Theatre, 100
Road America (Elkhart Lake), 136
Rocky Horror Picture Show, 105
Rocky Rococo's Pan-Style Pizza, 125, 128
rodeo, 73
roller skating, 83
R.T.A. Public Transportation Route Information (Chicago), 132
rugby, 83
Rummage-O-Rama, 108
Run For Your Heart, 83
running/jogging, 83

S

SAABGRAW, 75
Saddle Horse Show, American, 109
Safe House, The, 125
Safety Building, Milwaukee County, 55
sailing, 84
Sailing Center, Milwaukee Community, 84
sailing charters, 84
sailing clubs, 84
St. Hedwig's, 50, 51

St. Hyacinth's, 31, 32, 49
St. Joan of Arc Chapel, 22
St. Josaphat Basilica, 22, 33
St. Luke's Hospital tour, 57
St. Michael Hospital tour, 57
St. Paul's Episcopal Church, 98
St. Stanislaus Catholic Church, 35
Sts. Constantine and Helen Church, 90
Samson's Stomp, 70, 83
Sax Art Supplies, 120
Schlitz, Joseph, 15
Schlitz Audubon Center, 67, 82
School Sisters of Notre Dame, Convent of the, 32
Science and Industry, Museum of (Chicago), 134
Science Bag Lectures (UW-M), 108
Science, Economics and Technology Center, 19
Sciortino Bakery, 114
Sears, Roebuck and Company outlets, 117
Sears Tower (Chicago), 132
Second City (Chicago), 135
See-For-Yourself Auto Tour For Home Seekers, 27
Seigo's Japanese Steak House, 129
Selen's, 124
Sendik's Markets, 114
senior centers, 64
Seniors Only, 64
Serb Memorial Hall, 124
S.F.O., 119
Shakespeare, William, 142
Sheboygan, 138, 139, 142
Sheboygan County Museum, 139
Shedd Aquarium (Chicago), 133, 134
Sherman Boulevard, 38, 39, 42, 44
Shoots 'n' Roots, 68
shopping areas, 118, 119, 120
Shorewood Nature Preserve, 66, 82
Shorewood Players, 101
Shorewood Travel and Adventure Series, 105
Showbiz Pizza Place, 126, 127
Silver Lake Park (Kenosha), 86
Simma's Ovens Bakery, 114
Sinfonia Concertante, 98
Sing-It-Yourself *Messiah*, 95
skating, ice, 65, 82
skating, roller, 83
skiing, 84
skiing, cross-country, 67, 70, 84
skiing, downhill, 65, 85
Ski, Sky and Stage Show, Bartlett, 143

Skydivers/Parachute Club, Wisconsin, 110
Skylight Comic Opera Ltd., 88, 99
Sky Show (Chicago), 132
Snow Star Ski Club, 84, 85
soccer, 74, 85
Soccer Association, Wisconsin, 85
softball, 65, 75
Soldier's Home, 20
Southgate shopping center, 120
Southridge shopping center, 120
South Side Walking Tour, 29-36
South Stadium, 33
specialty shops, 121, 122
Spertus Museum of Judaica (Chicago), 134
Spheeris Sporting Goods, 122
Spice House, The, 114
Spiesegarten, 16, 125
Sports Collector Store, 121
Spotlight Series, 100
Spring Green, 142
Stand Rock Indian Ceremonial (Wisconsin Dells), 143
State Capitol, Wisconsin, 139
State Fair, Wisconsin, 92
State Fair Park, 80, 83, 88, 92, 108, 109
State Historical Society (Madison), 136, 137, 139, 140
State Parks, Wisconsin, 69, 131, 138, 141, 143
Steam Train (North Lake), 141
Stonecroft, 118
Stone Mill Winery, 14
Stonewood Village, 118
Storybook Gardens (Wisconsin Dells), 143
Streets of Old Milwaukee, 9
String Players Orchestra, Milwaukee, 96
Stroh's Run, 83
Sugar Plum Days, 10
Summer Concerts at St. Paul's, 98
Summer Evenings of Jewish Music, 98
Summerfest, 90
Sunset Playhouse, 88, 101
Super Run, 83
Sweet 'n' Counters, 114
Sweet Sensations, 114
swimming, 85
swimming pools, 65
Swiss Historical Village (New Glarus), 141
Symphony Band (UW-M), 99
Symphony Chorus, 99
Symphony Orchestra, Milwaukee, 70, 95, 97
Synagogue, 21

T

Taliesin, 142
Tanglewood, 126
Tanner Paull Post, 124
teatime, 25, 110
telephone numbers, box offices: Chicago, 135; Milwaukee, 88
television station tours, 60
tennis, 65, 86
Tesseract, 120
theater, 100-103
Theatre School Ltd., 100
Theatre X, 103
Three Brothers Bar and Restaurant, 127
Ticketcharge, 88
ticket office, Milwaukee County Stadium, 72, 73
Ticketron, 88
Tiffany, Louis Comfort, 4, 16, 20
Timber Wolf Farm, 110
Tivoli Gardens, 20
TLC Toys, 122
tobogganing, 65, 86
Todd Wehr Nature Center, 68
Tommy Bartlett Water Shows (Wisconsin Dells), 143
Tour About Inc., 26
tour companies, 25-27
Tourism, Wisconsin Division of, 84, 131
Tours D'Art, 26
Tower Hill State Park (Spring Green), 143
Trade Winds Spice Ltd., 114
Trading Post, 9, 11
train station tours, 58
Travel and Adventure film series, 105
Traveler's Aid (Chicago), 132
Travis Auction Galleries, 118
Trimborn Farm Park, 11
Truck and Tractor Pull Championship, 92
TubaChristmas, 95
Tyrannosaurus Rex, 5, 9

U

Uihlein Field, 73
Union Station (Chicago), 133
United Performing Arts Fund Open House, 20
University Art Museum, 107
University Book Store (Madison), 140
University of Wisconsin-Extension history tours, 26, 28
University of Wisconsin-Madison, 140
University of Wisconsin-Milwaukee:
  American Geographical Society Collection, 107
Art Galleries, 107
Box Offices, 88
College For Kids, 107
Craft Centre, 107
Elderhostel, 107
Films, 105
Fine Arts Department, 98
Greene Memorial Museum, 5
Olsen Planetarium, 108
Panthers, 74
Sailing Club, 84
Science Bag Lectures, 108
Union, 108
U.S. Coast Guard Auxiliary, 80
U.S. Postal Service tours, 61
U.S. Power Squadrons, 80
Usinger's Sausage Store, 114

V

Vagabond Ski Club, 75
Valley Power Plant tour, 61
Veterans Administration Medical Center, 20
Vilas Park Zoo (Madison), 140
Villa Terrace, 12
Visitor Information (Chicago), 132
Vocal Arts Consort, 99
vocal music, 99
Volkfest, 90
Von Steuben Monument, 39

W

Wade House Inn (Greenbush), 137
wading pools, 65
Waelderhaus (Kohler), 139
Walker's Point, 20
walking tours, 13, 27ff, 82, 140
Wanago Rodeo, 73
Ward Memorial Theatre/Liberace Playhouse, 20
Warriors, Marquette University, 72
Washington Park, 39, 97
water ski shows (Wisconsin Dells), 143
water slide, Noah's Ark (Wisconsin Dells), 143
Water Street, 119
Watertower Place (Chicago), 134
Watertower, Northpoint, 17
Watertown, 143
Watts, George, 110, 121

Waukesha Civic Theatre, 101
Waukesha County Historical Museum, 12
Waukesha Public Library, 69
Waukesha self-guided walking tour, 27
Waukesha Symphony Orchestra, 99
Wauwatosa, 27, 118
Wauwatosa Community Concert Association, 99
Wauwatosa Paramedics tours, 59
Wauwatosa Players, 101
Wauwatosa self-guided walking tour, 27
Wave, The, 74
Wehr Nature Center, 68
West Allis Farmer's Market, 114
West Allis Historical Society Museum, 13
West Allis Paramedics tours, 59
West Allis Players, 100
West Allis walking tour, 28
West Bank Cafe, 128
West Bend, 119
West Bend Company Outlet Store, 119
West Bend Factory Shopping Mall, 119
West Side Walking Tour, 38-45
Whitefish Bay Players, 101
Whitnall Park, 64
Wil-O-Way Centers, 64
Wilson Park, 64
Wind Ensemble (UW-M), 98
Wind Lake, 6
wind surfing, 86
Winton Sprengel House, 13
Wisconsin:
  Arabian Horse Show, 109
  Canoe Association, 80
  Conservatory of Music, 99
  Dells, 143
  Department of Natural Resources, 69, 81, 82
  Division of Tourism, 84, 131
  Electric Power Company tour, 61
  Gas Company tour, 61
  Go-Hikers, 82
  Handweaver's Show, 4
  Historical Society, 136, 137, 139, 140
  Kite Society, 83
  Linen, 119
  Outdoors Information, 84
  Skydivers/Parachute Club, 110
  Soccer Association, 85
  State Fair, 92
  State Fair Park, 80, 83, 88, 92, 108, 109
Wisconsin: Auto Tour Escapes, 131

Wisconsin Dells, 143
Wisconsin State Parks, 69, 131, 138, 141, 143
"Wisconsin: Winter Escape," 84
WISN-TV tour, 60
WITI-TV tour, 60
WMVS-TV 10/WMTV-TV 36 tour, 60
Woelke-Schultze Market, 114
Women's Rugby Football Club, Milwaukee, 83
Woodland Pattern, Inc. 110
Woods and Associates, Eleanor, 26
Woodwinds Arts Quintet (UW-M), 98
wrestling, 74
Wright, Frank Lloyd, 21, 26, 43, 90, 142
WTMJ-TV tour, 60
WVTV-TV tour, 60

Y

Yacht Club, Milwaukee, 84
YMCA, 81
Youth Orchestra, 97

Z

zoo concert series, 97
Zoo, Lincoln Park (Chicago), 133
Zoo, Milwaukee County, 70, 84
Zoo, Vilas Park (Madison), 140
Zoo, Racine, 142

About the Authors

Pamela Nonken was born and raised in Milwaukee. The mother of two teen-agers, she currently serves as a publicist for the Michael H. Lord Gallery. Her previous books include *The Allergy Cookbook and Food-Buying Guide,* coauthored with Dr. S. Roger Hirsch. Nonken has worked in recent years as a sales representative for *Milwaukee* magazine and the *Wisconsin Jewish Chronicle,* and as a publicist for *Milwaukee Epicure,* a guide featuring Milwaukee restaurants. A 1965 graduate of the University of Wisconsin, Nonken majored in speech and theater.

Nancy Luck moved to Milwaukee as a young mother. Her family now includes five children, from toddler to teen-ager. A former elementary school teacher, she now works as a Milwaukee representative for the West Coast firm of Peanut Butter Publishing. During 1983 and 1984, she served as the editor of *Milwaukee Epicure,* a Milwaukee restaurant guide. Following her graduation from the University of Wisconsin, in 1965, Luck studied art at Columbia University and Hunter College in New York City.

Barbara Smilow, a native of Washington, D.C., moved to Milwaukee in 1980 and immediately began exploring with her three children. Smilow previously taught elementary school in Pennsylvania and the District of Columbia, and offered cooking classes in Maryland. Following her graduation from the University of Maryland, in 1960, she studied art history at Temple University in Philadelphia and computer programming at Milwaukee Area Technical College. She is accomplished at making and flying kites. Smilow currently resides in Washington, D.C.

Also from Northword

FIRE & ICE *Don Davenport & Robert W. Wells*
Combines two deadly disaster epics under one cover. "These are shocking tales of nature's fury: the 1958 killer storm that sent the big ore carrier *Carl D. Bradley* bubbling to the bottom of Lake Michigan, and the 1871 holocaust that charred bodies and blackened the landscape in Peshtigo, Wisconsin, the most disastrous fire in American history.
"*Shipwreck on Lake Michigan*, by Don Davenport, a Great Lakes scholar, is the kind of story a reader can't put down. Robert Wells tells the searing story of *Fire at Peshtigo* with the sure hand of a veteran newspaperman." —*The Milwaukee Journal*
*$13.95 * 5½ x 8½, 450 pages, paper * ISBN 0-942802-04-7*

DAYLIGHT IN THE SWAMP! *Robert W. Wells*
This is history with the guts still in it — a boisterous yet realistic account of the men and women who came to the Northwoods of Wisconsin, Michigan, and Minnesota to make their living from logging. "This is heroic stuff."—*The New York Times*. "Documented by solid research. Recommended."—*Library Journal*. "A lively and colorful account of the heyday of lumbering in the Midwest that makes the old Wild West seem sedate. It's an entertaining piece of Americana."—*Publisher's Weekly*.
*$11.95 * 6 x 9, 240 pages, paper * ISBN 0-942802-07-1*

REMEMBERING THE WILDERNESS *Sara Rath*
Winner of the Banta Award for 1984. "The poems in this volume form an autobiography of sorts, a chronicle revealing what it is like to grow up in small town Wisconsin, to be married and divorced and married again, to give birth, to love, and to have sensual feelings that give life a particular zest and completeness. Sara Rath's poems show an appealing toughness, sensitivity, wit, and sensibility. They also offer a clear articulation of what being a fully sentient woman means in our present world."— *Wisconsin Academy Review*
*$6.95 * 5½ x 8½, 64 pages, paper * ISBN 0-942802-05-5*

ALL-SEASON GUIDE TO WISCONSIN'S PARKS *Jim Umhoefer*
"There are more than 70 state parks, forests, and trails in Wisconsin, and author Jim Umhoefer has visited them all. The guide is useful, informative, fun to read, and suited to all seasons, melding together commentary, maps, and photos. A browse through the book reveals the state's highest falls, best fishing holes — enjoyable regions to spend a few days. Bikers will find indispensable maps of the state's bike trails; hikers, campers, picnickers, vacationers, and anyone wanting to be outside will find this guide more than worth their money."—*Wisconsin Trails*
*$8.95 * 8½ x 11, 80 pages, paper * ISBN 0-942802-00-4*

ALL-SEASON GUIDE TO MINNESOTA'S PARKS *Jim Umhoefer*
"To assemble this information-rich guidebook, Jim Umhoefer traveled 12,000 miles in Minnesota, He camped, hiked, biked, backpacked, swam, canoed, sledded, skied and snowmobiled in discovering his adopted state. His book captures that intimacy, revealing little details and recounting anecdotes that underscore the charm of Minnesota's lakes, streams and forests. In Itasca State Park, for example, he pinpoints the bison kill site, locates bald eagles' nesting spots, and shows sunset fanciers where to watch the sun disappear as the haunting melody of loons drifts across the lake."—*The Milwaukee Journal*
*$9.95 * 8½ x 11, 104 pages, paper * ISBN 0-942802-06-3*

WISCONSIN SAMPLER *Sue E. McCoy, editor*
"A collection of remembrances and stories from the early 1900s by more than 40 Wisconsin writers. Some of the pieces come from the UW-Extension's Yarns of Yesteryear contest and others are by well known professionals such as Mel Ellis, Michael Goc, Justin Isherwood, and Sara Rath. All around, a finely crafted literary quilt."—*The Capital Times*
*$9.95 * 6 x 9, 204 pages, paper * ISBN 0-942802-03-9*

MARY CARTER: ON BEHALF OF THE AUNTS
I'L TELL YOU TOMORROW AND OTHER STORIES *Hazel Briggs*
I'll Tell You Tomorrow is a group of yarns about everyday people facing life in everyday situations; *Mary Carter* is a minor classic about a bunch of wacky but wonderful spinster sisters. "This collection spotlights the sprightly style and dry humor of Hazel Briggs. She may be in her mid 80s, but she's not lost her zest for life."—*The Milwaukee Journal*
Mary Carter @ *$4.95 * 5½ x 8½, 48 pages, paper * ISBN 0-942802-08-X*
I'll Tell You Tomorrow @ *$5.95 * 5½ x 8½, 104 pages, paper * ISBN 0-942802-01-2*